PROZAC

A MEDICAL DICTIONARY, BIBLIOGRAPHY,
AND ANNOTATED RESEARCH GUIDE TO
INTERNET REFERENCES

JAMES N. PARKER, M.D.
AND PHILIP M. PARKER, PH.D., EDITORS

ii

ICON Health Publications
ICON Group International, Inc.
4370 La Jolla Village Drive, 4th Floor
San Diego, CA 92122 USA

Printed in the United States of America.

Last digit indicates print number: 10 9 8 7 6 4 5 3 2 1

Publisher, Health Care: Philip Parker, Ph.D.
Editor(s): James Parker, M.D., Philip Parker, Ph.D.

Publisher's note: The ideas, procedures, and suggestions contained in this book are not intended for the diagnosis or treatment of a health problem. As new medical or scientific information becomes available from academic and clinical research, recommended treatments and drug therapies may undergo changes. The authors, editors, and publisher have attempted to make the information in this book up to date and accurate in accord with accepted standards at the time of publication. The authors, editors, and publisher are not responsible for errors or omissions or for consequences from application of the book, and make no warranty, expressed or implied, in regard to the contents of this book. Any practice described in this book should be applied by the reader in accordance with professional standards of care used in regard to the unique circumstances that may apply in each situation. The reader is advised to always check product information (package inserts) for changes and new information regarding dosage and contraindications before prescribing any drug or pharmacological product. Caution is especially urged when using new or infrequently ordered drugs, herbal remedies, vitamins and supplements, alternative therapies, complementary therapies and medicines, and integrative medical treatments.

Cataloging-in-Publication Data

Parker, James N., 1961-
Parker, Philip M., 1960-

Prozac: A Medical Dictionary, Bibliography, and Annotated Research Guide to Internet References / James N. Parker and Philip M. Parker, editors
        p.   cm.
Includes bibliographical references, glossary, and index.
ISBN: 0-597-83605-1
1. Prozac-Popular works.   I. Title.

Disclaimer

This publication is not intended to be used for the diagnosis or treatment of a health problem. It is sold with the understanding that the publisher, editors, and authors are not engaging in the rendering of medical, psychological, financial, legal, or other professional services.

References to any entity, product, service, or source of information that may be contained in this publication should not be considered an endorsement, either direct or implied, by the publisher, editors, or authors. ICON Group International, Inc., the editors, and the authors are not responsible for the content of any Web pages or publications referenced in this publication.

Copyright Notice

Acknowledgements

The collective knowledge generated from academic and applied research summarized in various references has been critical in the creation of this book which is best viewed as a comprehensive compilation and collection of information prepared by various official agencies which produce publications on Prozac. Books in this series draw from various agencies and institutions associated with the United States Department of Health and Human Services, and in particular, the Office of the Secretary of Health and Human Services (OS), the Administration for Children and Families (ACF), the Administration on Aging (AOA), the Agency for Healthcare Research and Quality (AHRQ), the Agency for Toxic Substances and Disease Registry (ATSDR), the Centers for Disease Control and Prevention (CDC), the Food and Drug Administration (FDA), the Healthcare Financing Administration (HCFA), the Health Resources and Services Administration (HRSA), the Indian Health Service (IHS), the institutions of the National Institutes of Health (NIH), the Program Support Center (PSC), and the Substance Abuse and Mental Health Services Administration (SAMHSA). In addition to these sources, information gathered from the National Library of Medicine, the United States Patent Office, the European Union, and their related organizations has been invaluable in the creation of this book. Some of the work represented was financially supported by the Research and Development Committee at INSEAD. This support is gratefully acknowledged. Finally, special thanks are owed to Tiffany Freeman for her excellent editorial support.

About the Editors

James N. Parker, M.D.

Dr. James N. Parker received his Bachelor of Science degree in Psychobiology from the University of California, Riverside and his M.D. from the University of California, San Diego. In addition to authoring numerous research publications, he has lectured at various academic institutions. Dr. Parker is the medical editor for health books by ICON Health Publications.

Philip M. Parker, Ph.D.

Philip M. Parker is the Eli Lilly Chair Professor of Innovation, Business and Society at INSEAD (Fontainebleau, France and Singapore). Dr. Parker has also been Professor at the University of California, San Diego and has taught courses at Harvard University, the Hong Kong University of Science and Technology, the Massachusetts Institute of Technology, Stanford University, and UCLA. Dr. Parker is the associate editor for ICON Health Publications.

About ICON Health Publications

To discover more about ICON Health Publications, simply check with your preferred online booksellers, including Barnes & Noble.com and Amazon.com which currently carry all of our titles. Or, feel free to contact us directly for bulk purchases or institutional discounts:

ICON Group International, Inc.
4370 La Jolla Village Drive, Fourth Floor
San Diego, CA 92122 USA
Fax: 858-546-4341
Web site: **www.icongrouponline.com/health**

Table of Contents

FORWARD

In March 2001, the National Institutes of Health issued the following warning: "The number of Web sites offering health-related resources grows every day. Many sites provide valuable information, while others may have information that is unreliable or misleading."[1] Furthermore, because of the rapid increase in Internet-based information, many hours can be wasted searching, selecting, and printing. Since only the smallest fraction of information dealing with Prozac is indexed in search engines, such as **www.google.com** or others, a non-systematic approach to Internet research can be not only time consuming, but also incomplete. This book was created for medical professionals, students, and members of the general public who want to know as much as possible about Prozac, using the most advanced research tools available and spending the least amount of time doing so.

In addition to offering a structured and comprehensive bibliography, the pages that follow will tell you where and how to find reliable information covering virtually all topics related to Prozac, from the essentials to the most advanced areas of research. Public, academic, government, and peer-reviewed research studies are emphasized. Various abstracts are reproduced to give you some of the latest official information available to date on Prozac. Abundant guidance is given on how to obtain free-of-charge primary research results via the Internet. **While this book focuses on the field of medicine, when some sources provide access to non-medical information relating to Prozac, these are noted in the text.**

E-book and electronic versions of this book are fully interactive with each of the Internet sites mentioned (clicking on a hyperlink automatically opens your browser to the site indicated). If you are using the hard copy version of this book, you can access a cited Web site by typing the provided Web address directly into your Internet browser. You may find it useful to refer to synonyms or related terms when accessing these Internet databases. **NOTE:** At the time of publication, the Web addresses were functional. However, some links may fail due to URL address changes, which is a common occurrence on the Internet.

For readers unfamiliar with the Internet, detailed instructions are offered on how to access electronic resources. For readers unfamiliar with medical terminology, a comprehensive glossary is provided. For readers without access to Internet resources, a directory of medical libraries, that have or can locate references cited here, is given. We hope these resources will prove useful to the widest possible audience seeking information on Prozac.

The Editors

---

[1] From the NIH, National Cancer Institute (NCI): **http://www.cancer.gov/cancerinfo/ten-things-to-know**.

CHAPTER 1. STUDIES ON PROZAC

Overview

In this chapter, we will show you how to locate peer-reviewed references and studies on Prozac.

Federally Funded Research on Prozac

The U.S. Government supports a variety of research studies relating to Prozac. These studies are tracked by the Office of Extramural Research at the National Institutes of Health.[2] CRISP (Computerized Retrieval of Information on Scientific Projects) is a searchable database of federally funded biomedical research projects conducted at universities, hospitals, and other institutions.

Search the CRISP Web site at **http://crisp.cit.nih.gov/crisp/crisp_query.generate_screen**. You will have the option to perform targeted searches by various criteria, including geography, date, and topics related to Prozac.

For most of the studies, the agencies reporting into CRISP provide summaries or abstracts. As opposed to clinical trial research using patients, many federally funded studies use animals or simulated models to explore Prozac. The following is typical of the type of information found when searching the CRISP database for Prozac:

- **Project Title: DOUBLE BLIND TRIAL OF ESTROGEN AUGMENTATION IN WOMEN W/ MAJOR DEPRESSION**

  Principal Investigator & Institution: Debattista, Charles; Stanford University Stanford, CA 94305

  Timing: Fiscal Year 2001

---

[2] Healthcare projects are funded by the National Institutes of Health (NIH), Substance Abuse and Mental Health Services (SAMHSA), Health Resources and Services Administration (HRSA), Food and Drug Administration (FDA), Centers for Disease Control and Prevention (CDCP), Agency for Healthcare Research and Quality (AHRQ), and Office of Assistant Secretary of Health (OASH).

Summary: The purpose of this study is to test the hypothesis that estrogen improves the response to fluoxetine (an antidepressant marketed in the U.S. as Prozac) in pre-menopausal women diagnosed with major depression. It is hoped that this study will provide information for more studies on the action and antidepressant effects of estrogen in depressed women. Approximately 120 subjects will participate in this study nationwide at 3 sites: Stanford University, Cornell University, and the University of Michigan. During the first phase of the study, subjects will be prescribed **Prozac** on a daily basis for 6 weeks. If a subject does not respond to the **Prozac** alone (meaning her depression symptoms are not significantly improved at the end of the 6 weeks), she will be eligible for the second phase of the study in which estrogen or placebo is added to the **Prozac** for an additional 4 weeks. This second phase is double-blind, meaning that neither the subject nor the investigators will know whether a subject is on estrogen or placebo. Subjects are evaluated on a regular basis and their depression symptoms and mental functions are assessed. Subjects will not be paid for participation in this part of the study. This part of the study will require approximately 8 visits, which last about 1 1/2 hours each. During the screening phase of this study, subjects are invited to participate in an additional brain imaging study. In this study, subjects receive a PET (Positive Emission Tomography) scan to evaluate changes in the use of sugar by the brain that occur with spontaneous, thought-triggered, and medication-triggered changes in subjects with depression. This may help us to better understand the changes in brain function that accompany different emotional states and to assess the possibility of using baseline brain function to more effectively target treatments in mood disorders. Subjects in this study will also receive an MRI (Magnetic Resonance Imaging) scan, a procedure that allows us to obtain detailed information about the structure of the brain by using magnetic and radiofrequency energy. Additionally, in order to test the hypothesis that the stress hormonal axis is more active in depressed patients, subjects will be administered metyrapone (a medication that temporarily blocks the production of cortisol) and blood samples will be drawn over the course of 6 hours. Subjects will also receive extensive neuropsychological testing that includes routine cognitive (intelligence, memory, and motor and perceptual processing) tests. Subjects who complete these additional studies will be paid $400 for their time. This part of the study will require approximately 5 long appointments.

Website: http://crisp.cit.nih.gov/crisp/Crisp_Query.Generate_Screen

- **Project Title: GENETIC ANALYSIS OF NEMATODE EGG LAYING**

  Principal Investigator & Institution: Horvitz, H R. Professor; Biology; Massachusetts Institute of Technology Cambridge, MA 02139

  Timing: Fiscal Year 2001; Project Start 01-JAN-1978; Project End 31-DEC-2004

  Summary: The long-term objective of this proposal is to understand how genes specify the structure, functioning and development of a behavioral system. Toward this end, the anatomically simple egg-laying system of the nematode Caenorhabditis elegans will be analyzed. Mutants abnormal in egg laying will be used to define both cells that act in egg laying and genes that control the development and functioning of those cells. Four distinct components of the egg-laying system will be analyzed: the vulva (through which eggs are laid); the egg-laying musculature; the nerve cells that directly control the egg-laying musculature; and nerve cells that indirectly regulate egg laying. Vulval development provides an excellent model for both intercellular signaling (how cells communicate) and morphogenesis (how cells generate complex three-dimensional structures). The studies of intercellular signaling in vulval development should reveal the normal biological functions and interactions of genes with human counterparts responsible for cancer. The studies of vulval morphogenesis focus on genes that are involved in the synthesis of specific carbohydrates and that appear to be similar to human genes involved in connective tissue disorders and aging. The contraction of muscles in general and of the C. elegans egg-laying muscles in particular requires the movement of ions through channels that span muscle membranes. The studies of the egg-laying musculature focus on a new class of ion channels and promise to establish new biological roles for ion channels and suggest candidate genes for diseases in which such channels are abnormal. Studies of the two classes of nerve cells (HSNs and VCs) that innervate the egg-laying muscles should help establish molecular genetic mechanisms responsible for many features of nerve cell development and activity, including the determination of cell identity, the outgrowth and branching of processes, and the formation and functioning of synapses (which allow communication between a nerve cell and its targets). Many genes involved in the development of these nerve cells have human counterparts associated with disease. Finally, nerve cells that control both egg laying and other behaviors, e.g., locomotion, will be identified and analyzed based on their effects on how the animal modulates its behavior in response to its environment and experience. Some of these cells communicate using the neurotransmitter serotonin, the target of major pharmaceutical agents used to treat depression -- **Prozac,** Paxil and Zoloft. In addition, how the environment and experience modulate behavior is a fundamental problem in neuroscience, and these studies should establish cellular and molecular mechanisms responsible for how sensory stimuli regulate behavior and how information about past experience is stored and retrieved.

Website: http://crisp.cit.nih.gov/crisp/Crisp_Query.Generate_Screen

- **Project Title: METHOD FOR MAKING AN IMPROVED ST JOHN'S WORT PRODUCT**

Principal Investigator & Institution: Castor, Trevor P. President & Chief Executive Officer; Aphios Corporation 3-E Gill St Woburn, MA 01801

Timing: Fiscal Year 2001; Project Start 30-SEP-1999; Project End 31-DEC-2002

Summary: (Adapted from the application): The goal of this Phase I/Phase II Fast Track project is to develop an improved St. John's Wort product which can be manufactured in a standardized and reproducible manner. St. John's Wort contains multiple bioactive compounds that have been used in a wide variety of ailments, most notably endogenous depression. The approach involves the use of supercritical fluids and near-critical fluids with and without polar cosolvents such as alcohols (trademarked as SuperFluids). These fluids are gases such as carbon dioxide which when compressed exhibit enhanced thermodynamic properties that can be fine-tuned for rapid and selective extraction of bioactive molecules. In Phase I, optimal conditions for selective SuperFluids extraction of and chromatographic purification of St. John's Wort will be established. In preliminary studies, this was accomplished by following the extraction of bioactive compounds with super critical carbon dioxide with 0 to 20% methanol. The results of Phase I studies will be used to develop a large scale manufacturing process. In a Phase II investigation, the conditions for selective extraction and chromatographic purification of bioactive compounds will be further optimized in terms of mechanical components, enhancement devices and operating parameters. Finally, it is proposed to design, build and test a pilot-scale prototype plant that could operate under cGMP conditions. Paracelsian (Ithaca, NY) will perform serotonin uptake assays on contract. PROPOSED COMMERCIAL APPLICATION: Among the most widely prescribed antidepressants in the United States are **Prozac** from Eli Lilly, Zoloft from Pfizer and Paxil from SmithKline Beecham. The worldwide sales of the top selling antidepressants are approximately $4.8

billion. As people experience adverse side-effects from prescription antidepressants, there has been a concomitant rise in the use of St. John's Wort and other herbs as natural anti- depressants. This Phase I/Phase II Fast Track SBIR project should lead to the development of a biologically-enhanced, stable and standardized St. John's Wort product that can be manufactured under cGMP conditions to provide a natural alternative with reduced side effects of **Prozac,** Pfizer and Paxil, and thus satisfy a burgeoning market demand in the $4.8 billion antidepressant marketplace.

Website: http://crisp.cit.nih.gov/crisp/Crisp_Query.Generate_Screen

- **Project Title: NEUROTRANSMITTER TRANSPORT**

Principal Investigator & Institution: Rudnick, Gary W. Professor; Pharmacology; Yale University 47 College Street, Suite 203 New Haven, CT 065208047

Timing: Fiscal Year 2001; Project Start 01-MAY-1993; Project End 31-JAN-2004

Summary: (Applicant's Abstract): Biogenic amine transporters are responsible for terminating the synaptic action of serotonin (5-HT), dopamine (DA), and norepinephrine (NE). They are the molecular targets for antidepressants such as imipramine and **Prozac** as well as for psychostimulants such as cocaine and amphetamines. Efforts currently directed at designing cocaine antagonists make assumptions about the proximity of cocaine and biogenic amine binding sites on the transporter. This application describes experiments designed to map the location of amino acid residues in biogenic amine transporters that are involved with substrate and inhibitor binding. These experiments will provide evidence to test the assumptions now being used to design cocaine treatment medications. Biogenic amine transporters use transmembrane ion gradients to drive neurotransmitter uptake. The coupling stoichiometry for this process is characteristic of each transporter. This proposal outlines plans to determine the ion coupling stoichiometry for DA transport and to compare it with the stoichiometry for NE and 5-HT transport. Mutant transporters will be tested to determine how the stoichiometry of an individual transporter depends on individual amino acids. Taken together, the experiments outlined in this proposal are directed toward the ultimate goal of understanding how each part of the primary sequence of a biogenic amine transport protein participates in the binding and the translocation of substrates.

Website: http://crisp.cit.nih.gov/crisp/Crisp_Query.Generate_Screen

- **Project Title: NEW APPROACHES TO MEMBRANE PROTEIN STRUCTURE**

Principal Investigator & Institution: Kaback, H R. Howard Hughes Medical Inst Investigator; Physiology; University of California Los Angeles 10920 Wilshire Blvd., Suite 1200 Los Angeles, CA 90024

Timing: Fiscal Year 2001; Project Start 01-JUN-1996; Project End 30-APR-2005

Summary: A highly significant percentage of the genomes sequenced thus far are thought to encode polytopic transmembrane proteins which catalyze a multitude of essential cellular functions, energy and signal transduction in particular. Many are important with regard to human disease (e.g. cystic fibrosis, drug resistance), and many widely prescribed drugs (eg. **Prozac** and Prilosec) are targeted to membrane transport proteins. Although progress over the last 20 years has led to the characterization, purification and modification of this class of proteins, only a few have been studied at a level useful for understanding mechanism. Furthermore, many membrane proteins require conformational flexibility in order to function, making it imperative to obtain dynamic structural information. The objectives of this application are to continue to utilize the lactose permease of Escherichia coli as a paradigm for structure/function studies on transmembrane proteins. Only 6 amino acid residues are irreplaceable with respect to mechanism, and application of novel site-directed biochemical and biophysical approaches has yielded a helix packing model to a resolution approximating 4 Angstrom units. Further efforts will be made to refine and extend the structure using these methods. In addition, newly developed approaches using site-directed fluorescence resonance energy transfer and solid-state 19F-NMR will be introduced. Ligand-induced conformational changes in certain helices can also be demonstrated, and these studies will be extended to the remainder of the molecule in order to delineate overall structural changes that result from ligand binding. The substrate binding site is located at the interface between helices IV and V, and specificity is directed towards the galactosyl moiety of the substrate. A spin-labeled galactoside that binds to the permease with high affinity has been synthesized and will be used to further define the substrate binding site. Ligands that bind but are not translocated are also being synthesized in order to study binding from the inner and outer surface of the membrane in the absence of translocation. Site-specific alkylation combined with mass spectrometry will be used to determine changes in the protonation of His322 (helix X) upon ligand binding.

Website: http://crisp.cit.nih.gov/crisp/Crisp_Query.Generate_Screen

- **Project Title: NON AMINES STRUCT ACTIVITY OF CARBATROPANES AT MONOAMINE TRANSPORTERS**

Principal Investigator & Institution: Madras, Bertha K. Professor; Harvard University (Medical School) Medical School Campus Boston, MA 02115

Timing: Fiscal Year 2001

Summary: Transporters for the monoamines dopamine, serotonin and norepinephrine are principal targets for the majority of antidepressant drugs such as fluoxetine/Prozac (serotonin transporter), methylphenidate/Ritalin (dopamine transporter), the most frequently prescribed drug for Attention Deficit Hyperactivity Disorder, and cocaine Without exception, the molecular structure of therapeutic and other drugs that modulate monoamine transporters contains an amine nitrogen We recently reported that the amine nitrogen can be exchanged for oxygen (aryloxatropanes, 8-oxa-bicyclo-3-aryl-[3 2 1]octanes) and retain potent inhibition of the dopamine, serotonin and/or norepinephrine transporters in monkey brain Oxygen-induced hydrogen bonding to substitute for amine-induced ionic bond formation was proposed as a mechanism to account for high affinity of this class of non-amines To investigate whether even hydrogen bonding is necessary, we replaced the oxygen with a carbon atom We now repo rt that several carbon-based compounds displayed high affinity binding for the dopamine transporter, including O-1231 (IC50 7 1 q 1 7nM), O-1414 (IC50 9 6 q 1 8 nM), O-1442 (IC50 14 3 q 1 1 nM) O-1231, which contains a flattened 2,3-unsaturated bond in the ring structure, was > 700-fold selective for the dopamine (DAT) over the serotonin (SERT) transporter O-1414, a saturated analog of O1231 in the 3- form ("chair") was only 3-fold selective for the DAT over the SERT whereas its 3-` analog ("boat") was > 10-fold Five conclusions can be drawn from these data Conformation of a molecule plays a significant role in conferring DAT or SERT affinity Orientation of the 3-aryl ring and the orientation of the 2-carbomethoxy ring relative to the aromatic ring is critical for alignment with the transporter Development of transporter-selective drug therapies for neuropsychiatric diseases can be guided by appropriate orientation of the 3-aryl group 8-Carbatropanes display high affinity for monoamine transporters, indicating that a functionality corresponding to an amine nitrogen is not necessary for anchoring the molecule to its target protein and blockade of monoamine transporters Within this series, transporter affinity appears to be largely sustained by the aromatic ring The DAT may have multiple binding sites for tropanes, while the SERT may be less flexible Ongoing research with mutant forms of the DAT will explore this premise This research has several implications First, it will clarify the feasibility of developing cocaine antagonists targeted to the dopamine transporter Second, it will help to clarify the molecular mechanisms by which drugs block monoamine transport Finally, these compounds have created a new generation of transporter drugs

Website: http://crisp.cit.nih.gov/crisp/Crisp_Query.Generate_Screen

- **Project Title: NOVEL REAGENTS AND CATALYSTS FOR CHIRAL PHARMACEUTICALS**

Principal Investigator & Institution: Soderquist, John A. Professor; University of Puerto Rico Rio Piedras Rio Piedras Sta San Juan, PR 00931

Timing: Fiscal Year 2001

Summary: Description (Adapted from Application): The project goals are directed toward the invention and development of novel, chiral, main-group organometallic reagents and catalysts for applications to the asymmetric synthesis of pharmaceuticals and natural products. The research focuses upon the chemistry of boron and silicon, which are generally both environmentally friendly and exhibit low toxicity. These structurally sound metalloidal systems provide defined stereochemical features, which can be utilized effectively in the synthetic and analytical operations commonly employed in the chemistry used in the health industry. Specific aims of the project include: (1) The design, synthesis, and evaluation of new types of chiral axazaborolanes and related catalysts for the borane-based catalytic asymmetric reduction of prochiral ketones. Constructed by a novel, intramolecular nitrogen-employing beta-azidoalkyl borinate esters and boranes, they have potential pharmaceutical applications (i.e., **Prozac,** D1 antagonists, beta-agonists, prostaglandins, thromboxane A2) by analogy to those of Corey's CBS catalysts, including the synthesis of anti-hypertensive drugs. Alternative catalysts based upon B-chiral borohydrides derived from diborons are also proposed. (2) Complementary to the above, new chiral potassium borohydride reagents are proposed, based upon the 10-trimethylsilyl-9-borabicyclo[3.3.2]decane ring system, which contain a B-chiral borohydride in a rigid system, a potentially versatile system for the asymmetric reduction of many ketone types. (3) Preliminary data also supports the feasibility of generating a wide variety of potassium aminoborohydrides through the simple reaction of aminoboranes with activated potassium hydride, a process which appears amenable to the synthesis of chiral potassium aminoborohydrides, systems which will also be examined as novel asymmetric reduction catalysts. (4) A new 11B-NMR protocol has been discovered which will be further developed as a highly effective, direct analysis of organoborane mixtures. Its utility in pharmaceutical applications has already been successful, providing a clear picture of the diastereomeric composition of the organoboranes employed in a drug synthesis, a finding that could have far-reaching significance for borane-based asymmetric processes. (5) Such technology has been utilized to prepare a new chiral silane derivatizing agent, which will be examined as a more versatile protocol than the Mosher ester method. (6) A new simple silane-based method for carboxylate protection will be applied to amino acids for potential applications to peptide and asymmetric synthesis.

Website: http://crisp.cit.nih.gov/crisp/Crisp_Query.Generate_Screen

- **Project Title: PHARMACOLOGY--ALLOSTERIC MODULATORS OF GABAA RECEPTORS**

  Principal Investigator & Institution: Guidotti, Alessandro; Professor; Psychiatry; University of Illinois at Chicago 1737 West Polk Street Chicago, IL 60612

  Timing: Fiscal Year 2001; Project Start 01-SEP-1992; Project End 30-NOV-2002

  Summary: (from applicant's abstract): The overall goal of our research project is to utilize the diversity of GABAalpha receptor structure and function to develop via new strategies safer and more effective neuroactive drugs acting as modulators of GABAalpha receptor function capable of anticonvulsant, anxiolytic, and antipanic action without eliciting tolerance or physical dependence. The present proposal is the continuation of an ongoing project aimed at understanding and further defining the role of "neurosteroids" in drug- induced positive and negative allosteric modulation of GABA action at GABAalpha receptors. The hypothesis of the proposed studies is that an increase of the GABAalpha receptor-active neurosteroid allopregnanolone (ALLO) elicited by fluoxetine or other SSRIs may be associated with the antidysphoric, anxiolytic, and anticonvulsant actions of this class of drugs. Because ALLO and related steroids acting at GABAalpha receptors play a putative role in modulating anxiety, mood, and cognitive behavior, to validate our hypothesis we need to establish whether the effect of SSRIs on neurosteroids is class-specific or whether other major classes of psychotherapeutic agents that act on mood and cognition (i.e., antidepressants, typical and atypical antipsychotics, benzodiazepines, cognition enhancers) alter neurosteroid biosynthesis and release. The focus on fluoxetine (Prozac), other serotonin reuptake inhibitors (SSRIs), and neurosteroids stems from our original observation that fluoxetine and other SSRIs increase the brain content of allopregnanolone (ALLO), which in nanomolar concentrations with nongenomic action positively modulates GABAalpha receptor function, and also decreases the brain content of 5alpha-dihydroprogesterone (5alpha- DHP), which also in nanomolar concentrations with genomic action (via progesterone receptors) may control GABAalpha receptor subunit gene expression. We propose a systematic investigation of the action of fluoxetine, other SSRIs, and other antidepressant and psychotherapeutic agents on brain neurosteroid biosynthesis and release with the following Specific Aims: (1) establish the onset and the duration of changes in ALLO and 5alpha- DHP content in various rat brain regions and microdialysates following administration of fluoxetine or other SSRIs; (2) determine if the increase of ALLO elicited by SSRIs is specific for this class of drugs; (3) establish if there is a correlation between the increase in brain and microdialysate ALLO content and the behavioral effects that reveal the strength of the underlying GABAergic transmission; (4) determine if the 33alpha-hydroxysteroid oxidoreductase enzymes are the target for fluoxetinee's action on neurosteroid treatment; and (5) study if neurosteroids alter GABAalpha receptor subunit expression following long-term fluoxetine treatment. Additional evidence that neurosteroid alterations are causally associated with SSRI drug treatment would enable a completely new insight into the development of safer and more efficacious antidepressants by focusing on their neurosteroidal actions.

  Website: http://crisp.cit.nih.gov/crisp/Crisp_Query.Generate_Screen

- **Project Title: PREPUBESCENT SSRIS & 5HT RECEPTOR SIGNALLING**

  Principal Investigator & Institution: Battaglia, George; Associate Professor; Pharmacol & Exper Therapeutics; Loyola University Medical Center Lewis Towers, 13Th Fl Chicago, IL 60611

  Timing: Fiscal Year 2001; Project Start 01-DEC-1999; Project End 30-NOV-2003

Summary: Fluoxetine (Prozac) and other serotonin-selective reuptake blockers (SSRIs) are being increasingly used to treat mood disorders in children. In adults, fluoxetine increases postsynaptic 5HT2A receptor signalling. In contrast, our data reveal that when administered prior to maturation, fluoxetine 5HT2A receptor signal transduction, an effect that is opposite to that produced in adults. However, virtually no preclinical data exist regarding the immediate or long-term changes in 5HT systems due to prepubescent SSRI treatment. The long-term objective of this proposal is to understand the mechanisms and persistence of adaptive changes in 5HT receptor systems produced by pubescent exposure to SSRIs. Because the clinical effectiveness of SSRIs is associated with adaptive changes in 5HT signal transduction, our HYPOTHESIS is that (1) prepubescent fluaxetine treatment will produce different neuroadaptations in postsynaptic 5HT1A and 5HT2A signal transduction than produced by adult treatment, and (2) the effects of prepubescent SSRIs will persist into adulthood and consequently, alter the ability of 5HT systems to respond to subsequent SSRI administration during adulthood. Aim 1 will determine the dose-dependence of fluoxetine-induced changes in postsynaptic 5HT1A and 5HT2A receptors and receptor-mediated neuroendocrine responses, and will establish the treatment dose for subsequent studies. Aim 2 will determine the biochemical mechanisms responsible for fluoxetine-induced adaptation(s) in postsynaptic 5HT1A and 5HT2A receptor systems, by investigating changes in specific components of the signal transduction pathway between 5HT receptors and their respective second messenger enzymes. Aim 3 and Aim 4 will investigate the longer-term effects of prepubescent fluoxetine treatment on changes in postsynaptic 5HT signal transduction. Postsynaptic 5HT1A (aim 3) and 5HT2A (aim 4) receptor systems will be studied with respect to: (1) the persistence of prepubescent fluoxetine-induced 5HT adaptations into adulthood and (2) the regulation of 5HT receptor systems in response to subsequent adult fluoxetine administration following prepubescent exposure. These studies will provide important new information about the mechanisms underlying the immediate and long-term adaptive changes in brain 5HT signalling due to prepubescent fluoxetine treatment. These studies will also elucidate the status of serotonergic function in adults treated previously with SSRIs as juveniles in order to predict how these individuals will respond to subsequent antidepressant treatment as adults. This information is critical to the effective use of SSRIs in treating mood disorders in children and in treating adults treated previously with SSRIs as juveniles.

Website: http://crisp.cit.nih.gov/crisp/Crisp_Query.Generate_Screen

- **Project Title: ROLE OF SEROTONIN IN OSTEOCLAST DIFFERENTATION**

  Principal Investigator & Institution: Stashenko, Philip P. Vice President for Research; Forsyth Institute Boston, MA 02115

  Timing: Fiscal Year 2003; Project Start 01-JUL-1997; Project End 31-MAY-2006

  Summary: (provided by applicant): Recent findings suggest that regulatory interactions occur between the neural and skeletal systems. Using DNA microarrays, we found that expression of the serotonin transporter (5-HTT) is strongly up-regulated in RANKL-induced osteoclasts (OC). Fluoxetine ('Prozac'), a selective 5-HTT inhibitor, dose-dependently inhibited OC formation and resorptive activity. Mice homozygous for a deletion of the 5-htt gene exhibited increased cortical bone mass, and fluoxetine treatment of Swiss-Webster mice increased trabecular bone. These findings lead to the novel hypothesis that the serotonin (5-HT) system plays a crucial role in bone formation and remodeling, via effects on osteoclast development and/or activation. Aim 1 will characterize the expression of elements of the serotonin system in osteoclasts (OC) at the mRNA and protein levels, and will confirm that each is functional. Aim 2 will determine the role of serotonin (5-HT), the 5-HTT, serotonin receptors (SIR), vesicular monoamine transporter 1 (VMAT1), and monoamine oxidase (MAO) A in the formation and/or activation of OC in vitro, using a panel of specific agonists and inhibitors. In Aim 3, we will test the hypothesis that elevations in intracellular 5-HT are necessary for the observed effects, via effects on RANK-stimulated NFkB activation. Aim 4 will analyze the roles of the 5-HTT, SIRs, VMAT1, and MAO A in osteoclastogenesis in vivo using appropriate knockout mice. Aim 5 will determine the function of these serotonin system components in models of pathologic bone resorption, including resorption caused by estrogen-depletion or infection. The goal is to characterize the elements of the serotonin system that are present in OC, and determine their role in the regulation of bone mass under physiologic and pathologic conditions.

Website: http://crisp.cit.nih.gov/crisp/Crisp_Query.Generate_Screen

- **Project Title: STRESS-INDUCED REORGANIZATION OF THE AMYGDALA**

Principal Investigator & Institution: Salm, Adrienne K. Professor; Anatomy; West Virginia University P. O. Box 6845 Morgantown, WV 265066845

Timing: Fiscal Year 2001; Project Start 01-MAR-2000; Project End 28-FEB-2003

Summary: (applicant's abstract): More than 23 million Americans suffer from clinically significant anxiety and depressive disorders, some 20 million Americans abuse illicit drugs and over 7 percent of the population are dependent on or abuse alcohol. Stress appears to have exacerbating effects on these psychological conditions and may be an etiological factor as well. The aim of this research is to determine the mechanisms underlying the brain's vulnerability to environmental stress, which lead to chronic fear and anxiety. In particular, we will pursue biochemical and behavioral studies from our laboratories that have established that, in the rat, maternal stress during gestation (prenatal stress) reliably creates offspring which, as adults, 1) exhibit increased fear in a stressful situation, 2) have increased levels of the anxiogenic neuropeptide, corticotropin-releasing factor (CRF), in the amygdala, and 3) have an enlarged amygdala, brought about, at least in part, by an increase in the numbers of neurons and glia. Much evidence has linked the amygdala and CRF to the control of emotional behavior. We hypothesize that the amygdala undergoes structural and neurochemical plasticity in response to stress, and that these changes account for the vulnerability to stress that underlies increased fearfulness. Three specific aims are proposed: 1) to make stereologic measures of amygdaloid volume and cell numbers, autoradiographic measures of CRF receptors, and behavioral measures of hyper-responsiveness to acute stress in normal and prenatally stressed (PS) rats early in development and throughout life, 2) to determine if interventions that will reduce stress during relevant developmental periods will affect normal rats, and ameliorate the accompanying anatomical, biochemical and behavioral changes that occur in PS rats, 3) to determine if the development of hyper-responsiveness to stress in adult rats in response to chronic, daily stressors is accompanied by biochemical and structural reorganization of the amygdala, and 3b) to determine in adult rates if treatment with the anxiolytic drug fluoxetine (Prozac) can block chronic stress- and prenatal stress-induced hyperresponsiveness and changes in amygdaloid volume, cell numbers, and CRF receptors. Determining the differences in the brains of animals that exhibit variations in vulnerability to stress will identify neurobiological mechanisms that lead to anxiety disorders, depression, and drug abuse, and provide new directions for the diagnosis and treatment of stress-related diseases and mental illness.

Website: http://crisp.cit.nih.gov/crisp/Crisp_Query.Generate_Screen

- **Project Title: SYNERGY BETWEEN SSRIS AND OVARIAN HORMONES**

Principal Investigator & Institution: Van De Kar, Louis D. Professor; Pharmacol & Exper Therapeutics; Loyola University Medical Center Lewis Towers, 13Th Fl Chicago, IL 60611

Timing: Fiscal Year 2001; Project Start 05-AUG-1999; Project End 31-JUL-2004

Summary: Women suffer from disorders associated with serotonin (5-HT) deficiency, such as premenstrual syndrome (PMS) post-partum and post-menopausal depression, anxiety and bulimia. These mood and impulse control disorders are also associated with fluctuations in ovarian hormone levels. Estrogen can be used to treat some of these disorders, but serotonin reuptake inhibitors (SSRIs), such as fluoxetine (Prozac) are the most effective drugs currently available. A major problem with SSRIs is the delay (2-3 weeks) in onset of clinical improvement of depression, a time which is associated with increased danger of suicide. Treatment with either fluoxetine or estrogen decreases the sensitivity of hypothalamic 5-HT1A receptor systems. These observations suggest that desensitization of 5-HT1A receptor signalling may underlie the therapeutic effectiveness of estrogen and SSRI treatments. Ovarian hormones act predominantly via genomic mechanisms, while fluoxetine induces adaptive responses via membrane proteins. Therefore, our central hypothesis is that estrogen will act synergistically with fluoxetine via complementary mechanisms to desensitize hypothalamic 5-HT1A receptor systems. Based on this hypothesis, we predict that estrogen or estrogen + progesterone will shorten the delay in the effects of SSRIs. The proposed studies will examine the mechanisms by which estrogen: 1) inhibits 5-HT1A signal transduction systems, and 2) reduces the delay in fluoxetine-induced desensitization of hypothalamic 5-HT1A receptor signalling. The proposed studies will use neuroendocrine, biochemical and molecular approaches to study the following specific aims: Specific Aim 1 will determine the doses of estrogen and progesterone that reduce hypothalamic 5-HT1A receptor function in ovariectomized rats. Specific Aim 2 will identify the estrogen receptor subtype(s) which mediate the effect of estrogen on 5-HT1A receptor systems in the hypothalamus. Specific Aim 3 will determine if estrogen shortens the delay in fluoxetine's effects on 5-HT1A receptor signalling. Specific Aim 4 will determine if progesterone increases estrogen's effectiveness in shortening the delay in fluoxetine-induced 5-HT1A receptor sub-sensitivity. The proposed studies will provide the scientific basis for the development of improved therapeutic regimens and novel drugs that provide faster clinical improvement in women suffering from PMS, depression, bulimia and anxiety disorders.

Website: http://crisp.cit.nih.gov/crisp/Crisp_Query.Generate_Screen

- **Project Title: SYNTHESIS OF FLUOXETINE ANALOGS: SUBSTITUTED BENZAZEPINE**

Principal Investigator & Institution: Okoro, Cosmas O.; Tennessee State University 3500 Centennial Blvd Nashville, TN 37203

Timing: Fiscal Year 2003; Project Start 01-JAN-2003; Project End 31-DEC-2006

Summary: Fluoxetine (Prozac) is a commonly prescribed antidepressant that targets the serotonin transporter. Unlike tricyclics, such as imipramine, fluoxetine has little effect on other receptors, resulting in a lower occurrence of sedative and cardiovascular side effects. The semi-rigid sertraline (Zoloft) has a mechanism similar to fluoxetine, but is superior, because it confers lesser sedation than fluoxetine, in addition to being short acting. The primary objective of the present study is the design and synthesis of conformationally-restricted derivatives of fluoxetine, as potential pharmacologically active compounds. Both (R) and (S)-fluoxetine are flexible molecules. The (S)-isomer displays prolonged duration in man, which may contribute to side effects. Flexible molecules may have more than one site of action, with one preferred conformation at the receptor site. Side effects observed may be due to a low-energy conformation of fluoxetine at a second site. The synthesis of analogs in which the molecular framework of the pharmacophore is "locked" into semi-rigid form will allow a full study of the conformational aspects of drug action. The consideration of a benzazepine moiety in the proposed compounds was made in the light of cyclized version of norfluoxetine, which is active. Although amphetamines, cocaine and antidepressants profoundly affect human behavior, their underlyling mechanisms of action are unknown. It is postulated that the interactions of antidepressants with transporters account for the primary action of these drugs. The synthesized compounds will be used to study neurotransmitter uptake mechanisms, i.e. how transporters clear transmitters from the synaptic cleft after they are released from the nerve terminal. This part of the work will be done in colloboration with Dr. Louis J. DeFelice, Professor of Pharmacology and Neuroscience at Vanderbilt University School of Medicine. The research project will ultimately provide novel compounds for the treatment of depression and mental illness.

Website: http://crisp.cit.nih.gov/crisp/Crisp_Query.Generate_Screen

- **Project Title: TRAFFICKING AND REGULATION OF MONOAMINE TRANSPORTERS**

Principal Investigator & Institution: Melikian, Haley E. Assistant Professor; Psychiatry; Univ of Massachusetts Med Sch Worcester Office of Research Funding Worcester, MA 01655

Timing: Fiscal Year 2002; Project Start 01-MAY-2002; Project End 30-APR-2007

Summary: (provided by applicant): Monoamine reuptake is a major mechanism for regulating extraneuronal monoamine levels and terminating synaptic transmission. Reuptake is mediated by plasma membrane transporters that are the primary targets for psychostimulants such as cocaine, methamphetamine and MDMA ("Ecstasy"), as well as for therapeutic drugs such as fuoxetine (Prozac), sibutramine (Meridia), bupropion (Wellbutrin) and methylphenidate (Ritalin). These agents block reuptake, resulting in elevated extraneuronal monoamine levels and enhanced postsynaptic responses. Recent evidence demonstrates that transporters are subject to acute regulation by cellular signaling pathways. Transporter regulation is coupled to dynamic changes in transporter cell-surface presentation, suggesting that membrane trafficking is fundamental to transporter homeostasis and regulation. However, the cellular and molecular mechanisms governing transporter regulation and trafficking are not yet defined. Given the pronounced effect pharmacological transporter blockade exerts on synaptic transmission, it is highly likely that transporter sequestration also has significant downstream effects on neuronal signaling. Moreover, modulation of transporter availability is certain to have significant impact on the efficacy of psychoactive drugs. The major goals of this project are to elucidate the cellular and molecular mechanisms mediating acute transporter regulation and trafficking. This investigative line will be pursued by testing the following hypotheses: (1) Transporters undergo constitutive internalization and recycling, and (2) transporter regulation is achieved by altering transporter trafficking kinetics. These hypotheses are based on strong preliminary data that the dopamine transporter (DAT) undergoes constitutive endosomal trafficking and that protein kinase C (PKC) activation directly alters DAT trafficking. The proposed hypotheses will be tested by directly analyzing basal and regulated transporter trafficking kinetics in cell lines. Intrinsic domains mediating basal and PKC-regulated DAT trafficking will be identified using molecular truncation and mutagenesis approaches. It is expected that these approaches will provide a clear and comprehensive picture of the mechanisms underlying acute transporter modulation. Such results are expected to have a significant impact on future therapeutic strategies aimed at monoamine-related drug abuse and mental illnesses. Moreover, the outcomes will greatly improve our understanding of the factors contributing to monoamine availability and signaling in the brain.

Website: http://crisp.cit.nih.gov/crisp/Crisp_Query.Generate_Screen

E-Journals: PubMed Central[3]

PubMed Central (PMC) is a digital archive of life sciences journal literature developed and managed by the National Center for Biotechnology Information (NCBI) at the U.S. National Library of Medicine (NLM).[4] Access to this growing archive of e-journals is free and unrestricted.[5] To search, go to **http://www.ncbi.nlm.nih.gov/entrez/query.fcgi?db=Pmc**, and type "Prozac" (or synonyms) into the search box. This search gives you access to full-text articles. The following is a sample of items found for Prozac in the PubMed Central database:

- **Blockage of 5HT2C serotonin receptors by fluoxetine (Prozac).** by Ni YG, Miledi R. 1997 Mar 4;
  http://www.pubmedcentral.gov/articlerender.fcgi?tool=pmcentrez&artid=20038

- **Blockage of muscle and neuronal nicotinic acetylcholine receptors by fluoxetine (Prozac).** by Garcia-Colunga J, Awad JN, Miledi R. 1997 Mar 4;
  http://www.pubmedcentral.gov/articlerender.fcgi?tool=pmcentrez&artid=20039

- **Involvement of striatal and extrastriatal DARPP-32 in biochemical and behavioral effects of fluoxetine (Prozac).** by Svenningsson P, Tzavara ET, Witkin JM, Fienberg AA, Nomikos GG, Greengard P. 2002 Mar 5;
  http://www.pubmedcentral.gov/articlerender.fcgi?tool=pmcentrez&artid=122493

The National Library of Medicine: PubMed

One of the quickest and most comprehensive ways to find academic studies in both English and other languages is to use PubMed, maintained by the National Library of Medicine.[6] The advantage of PubMed over previously mentioned sources is that it covers a greater number of domestic and foreign references. It is also free to use. If the publisher has a Web site that offers full text of its journals, PubMed will provide links to that site, as well as to

---

[3] Adapted from the National Library of Medicine: **http://www.pubmedcentral.nih.gov/about/intro.html**.

[4] With PubMed Central, NCBI is taking the lead in preservation and maintenance of open access to electronic literature, just as NLM has done for decades with printed biomedical literature. PubMed Central aims to become a world-class library of the digital age.

[5] The value of PubMed Central, in addition to its role as an archive, lies in the availability of data from diverse sources stored in a common format in a single repository. Many journals already have online publishing operations, and there is a growing tendency to publish material online only, to the exclusion of print.

[6] PubMed was developed by the National Center for Biotechnology Information (NCBI) at the National Library of Medicine (NLM) at the National Institutes of Health (NIH). The PubMed database was developed in conjunction with publishers of biomedical literature as a search tool for accessing literature citations and linking to full-text journal articles at Web sites of participating publishers. Publishers that participate in PubMed supply NLM with their citations electronically prior to or at the time of publication.

sites offering other related data. User registration, a subscription fee, or some other type of fee may be required to access the full text of articles in some journals.

To generate your own bibliography of studies dealing with Prozac, simply go to the PubMed Web site at **http://www.ncbi.nlm.nih.gov/pubmed**. Type "Prozac" (or synonyms) into the search box, and click "Go." The following is the type of output you can expect from PubMed for Prozac (hyperlinks lead to article summaries):

- **"There is nothing in this world can make me joy". Fluoxetine (Prozac) poisoning.**
  Author(s): Mack RB.
  Source: N C Med J. 1994 August; 55(8): 358-60. No Abstract Available.
  http://www.ncbi.nlm.nih.gov:80/entrez/query.fcgi?cmd=Retrieve&db=PubMed&list_
  uids=7935885&dopt=Abstract

- **A question about Prozac and arthralgias.**
  Author(s): Stalheim RM.
  Source: N C Med J. 1990 April; 51(4): 186-7. No Abstract Available.
  http://www.ncbi.nlm.nih.gov:80/entrez/query.fcgi?cmd=Retrieve&db=PubMed&list_
  uids=2333115&dopt=Abstract

- **Akathisia causing suicide attempts in patients taking fluoxetine (Prozac)**
  Author(s): Tueth MJ.
  Source: The Journal of Emergency Medicine. 1993 May-June; 11(3): 336-7.
  http://www.ncbi.nlm.nih.gov:80/entrez/query.fcgi?cmd=Retrieve&db=PubMed&list_
  uids=8340595&dopt=Abstract

- **American institute for psychoanalysis. The president and Prozac.**
  Author(s): Rubin J.
  Source: American Journal of Psychoanalysis. 1994 March; 54(1): 95-7.
  http://www.ncbi.nlm.nih.gov:80/entrez/query.fcgi?cmd=Retrieve&db=PubMed&list_
  uids=8203662&dopt=Abstract

- **Backfire. Could Prozac and Elavil promote tumor growth?**
  Author(s): Nemecek S.
  Source: Scientific American. 1994 September; 271(3): 22-3.
  http://www.ncbi.nlm.nih.gov:80/entrez/query.fcgi?cmd=Retrieve&db=PubMed&list_
  uids=8091186&dopt=Abstract

- **Been down so long. Prozac and other new drugs triggered a revolution in the treatment of depression. But do we still need the couch?**
  Author(s): Gupta S.
  Source: Time. 2002 January 21; 159(3): 148.
  http://www.ncbi.nlm.nih.gov:80/entrez/query.fcgi?cmd=Retrieve&db=PubMed&list_
  uids=11833124&dopt=Abstract

- **Blockage of 5HT2C serotonin receptors by fluoxetine (Prozac).**
  Author(s): Ni YG, Miledi R.
  Source: Proceedings of the National Academy of Sciences of the United States of America. 1997 March 4; 94(5): 2036-40.
  http://www.ncbi.nlm.nih.gov:80/entrez/query.fcgi?cmd=Retrieve&db=PubMed&list_
  uids=9050900&dopt=Abstract

- **Can Prozac cut health costs?**
  Author(s): Smith L.
  Source: Fortune. 1997 May 12; 135(9): 28, 30.
  http://www.ncbi.nlm.nih.gov:80/entrez/query.fcgi?cmd=Retrieve&db=PubMed&list_uids=10167285&dopt=Abstract

- **Concern over Prozac-induced tumor growth may dwindle following FDA study.**
  Author(s): Mathews J.
  Source: Journal of the National Cancer Institute. 1995 September 6; 87(17): 1285-7.
  http://www.ncbi.nlm.nih.gov:80/entrez/query.fcgi?cmd=Retrieve&db=PubMed&list_uids=7658480&dopt=Abstract

- **Development of antidepressant drugs. Fluoxetine (Prozac) and other selective serotonin uptake inhibitors.**
  Author(s): Wong DT, Bymaster FP.
  Source: Advances in Experimental Medicine and Biology. 1995; 363: 77-95. Review.
  http://www.ncbi.nlm.nih.gov:80/entrez/query.fcgi?cmd=Retrieve&db=PubMed&list_uids=7618533&dopt=Abstract

- **Enantiomeric separation and quantification of fluoxetine (Prozac) in human plasma by liquid chromatography/tandem mass spectrometry using liquid-liquid extraction in 96-well plate format.**
  Author(s): Shen Z, Wang S, Bakhtiar R.
  Source: Rapid Communications in Mass Spectrometry : Rcm. 2002; 16(5): 332-8.
  http://www.ncbi.nlm.nih.gov:80/entrez/query.fcgi?cmd=Retrieve&db=PubMed&list_uids=11857715&dopt=Abstract

- **First-trimester exposure to fluoxetine (prozac). Does it affect pregnancy outcome?**
  Author(s): Koren G.
  Source: Can Fam Physician. 1996 January; 42: 43-4. No Abstract Available.
  http://www.ncbi.nlm.nih.gov:80/entrez/query.fcgi?cmd=Retrieve&db=PubMed&list_uids=8924812&dopt=Abstract

- **Fluoxetine (Prozac)**
  Author(s): Gillman PK.
  Source: The Medical Journal of Australia. 1993 October 4; 159(7): 492.
  http://www.ncbi.nlm.nih.gov:80/entrez/query.fcgi?cmd=Retrieve&db=PubMed&list_uids=8412933&dopt=Abstract

- **Fluoxetine (Prozac) as a cause of QT prolongation.**
  Author(s): Varriale P.
  Source: Archives of Internal Medicine. 2001 February 26; 161(4): 612.
  http://www.ncbi.nlm.nih.gov:80/entrez/query.fcgi?cmd=Retrieve&db=PubMed&list_uids=11252125&dopt=Abstract

- **Fluoxetine (Prozac) interference in CN column liquid-chromatographic assays of tricyclic antidepressants and metabolites.**
  Author(s): Puopolo PR, Flood JC.
  Source: Clinical Chemistry. 1991 July; 37(7): 1304-5.
  http://www.ncbi.nlm.nih.gov:80/entrez/query.fcgi?cmd=Retrieve&db=PubMed&list_uids=1855312&dopt=Abstract

- **Fluoxetine (Prozac): a profile and clinical recommendations.**
  Author(s): Favazza AR.
  Source: Mo Med. 1991 January; 88(1): 25-7. No Abstract Available.
  http://www.ncbi.nlm.nih.gov:80/entrez/query.fcgi?cmd=Retrieve&db=PubMed&list_uids=1994238&dopt=Abstract

- **Fluoxetine hydrochloride (Prozac) toxicity in a neonate.**
  Author(s): Spencer MJ.
  Source: Pediatrics. 1993 November; 92(5): 721-2.
  http://www.ncbi.nlm.nih.gov:80/entrez/query.fcgi?cmd=Retrieve&db=PubMed&list_uids=8414864&dopt=Abstract

- **Fluoxetine hydrochloride (Prozac)-induced pulmonary disease.**
  Author(s): Gonzalez-Rothi RJ, Zander DS, Ros PR.
  Source: Chest. 1995 June; 107(6): 1763-5.
  http://www.ncbi.nlm.nih.gov:80/entrez/query.fcgi?cmd=Retrieve&db=PubMed&list_uids=7781383&dopt=Abstract

- **Frankenstein in the age of Prozac.**
  Author(s): Goodson AC.
  Source: Literature and Medicine. 1996 Spring; 15(1): 16-32.
  http://www.ncbi.nlm.nih.gov:80/entrez/query.fcgi?cmd=Retrieve&db=PubMed&list_uids=8728276&dopt=Abstract

- **Freud, Prozac, and the human condition.**
  Author(s): Khouzam HR.
  Source: Canadian Journal of Psychiatry. Revue Canadienne De Psychiatrie. 1996 April; 41(3): 195.
  http://www.ncbi.nlm.nih.gov:80/entrez/query.fcgi?cmd=Retrieve&db=PubMed&list_uids=8722653&dopt=Abstract

- **Generation prozac.**
  Author(s): Grodeck B.
  Source: Posit Aware. 1995 May-June; : 18-9.
  http://www.ncbi.nlm.nih.gov:80/entrez/query.fcgi?cmd=Retrieve&db=PubMed&list_uids=11362374&dopt=Abstract

- **Growth failure associated with the use of high dose prozac (fluoxetine hydrochloride) in a patient with type 1 diabetes mellitus.**
  Author(s): Frank GR, Navon RE.
  Source: J Pediatr Endocrinol Metab. 1999 May-June; 12(3): 467-9. No Abstract Available.
  http://www.ncbi.nlm.nih.gov:80/entrez/query.fcgi?cmd=Retrieve&db=PubMed&list_uids=10821228&dopt=Abstract

- **How Barr managed to kill Eli Lilly's patent on Prozac.**
  Author(s): Pabst PL.
  Source: Tissue Engineering. 2001 December; 7(6): 843-4.
  http://www.ncbi.nlm.nih.gov:80/entrez/query.fcgi?cmd=Retrieve&db=PubMed&list_uids=11749739&dopt=Abstract

- **If everyone were on Prozac.**
  Author(s): Gupta S.
  Source: Time. 2003 January 20; 161(3): 81.
  http://www.ncbi.nlm.nih.gov:80/entrez/query.fcgi?cmd=Retrieve&db=PubMed&list_uids=12545568&dopt=Abstract

- **Imaging stroke recovery: lessons from Prozac.**
  Author(s): Detre JA.
  Source: Annals of Neurology. 2001 December; 50(6): 697-8.
  http://www.ncbi.nlm.nih.gov:80/entrez/query.fcgi?cmd=Retrieve&db=PubMed&list_uids=11761466&dopt=Abstract

- **In our streams: Prozac and pesticides.**
  Author(s): Lemonick MD.
  Source: Time. 2003 August 25; 162(8): 51.
  http://www.ncbi.nlm.nih.gov:80/entrez/query.fcgi?cmd=Retrieve&db=PubMed&list_uids=12964463&dopt=Abstract

- **Is Prozac really perilous?**
  Author(s): Lang DA.
  Source: Minn Med. 1995 March; 78(3): 2-3. No Abstract Available.
  http://www.ncbi.nlm.nih.gov:80/entrez/query.fcgi?cmd=Retrieve&db=PubMed&list_uids=7739475&dopt=Abstract

- **It's Prozac time in medicine.**
  Author(s): Heilman RS.
  Source: Radiographics : a Review Publication of the Radiological Society of North America, Inc. 1996 September; 16(5): 996.
  http://www.ncbi.nlm.nih.gov:80/entrez/query.fcgi?cmd=Retrieve&db=PubMed&list_uids=8888386&dopt=Abstract

- **Listening to Prozac.**
  Author(s): Walder J.
  Source: Nature. 1994 May 19; 369(6477): 178.
  http://www.ncbi.nlm.nih.gov:80/entrez/query.fcgi?cmd=Retrieve&db=PubMed&list_uids=8183333&dopt=Abstract

- **Listening to Prozac.**
  Author(s): Kaplan R.
  Source: Nature. 1994 May 19; 369(6477): 178.
  http://www.ncbi.nlm.nih.gov:80/entrez/query.fcgi?cmd=Retrieve&db=PubMed&list_uids=8183332&dopt=Abstract

- **Listening to Prozac.**
  Author(s): Freeman H.
  Source: Nature. 1994 May 19; 369(6477): 178.
  http://www.ncbi.nlm.nih.gov:80/entrez/query.fcgi?cmd=Retrieve&db=PubMed&list_
  uids=8183331&dopt=Abstract

- **Mass media representations as drug information for patients: the prozac phenomenon.**
  Author(s): Montagne M.
  Source: Substance Use & Misuse. 2001 July-August; 36(9-10): 1261-74.
  http://www.ncbi.nlm.nih.gov:80/entrez/query.fcgi?cmd=Retrieve&db=PubMed&list_
  uids=11592472&dopt=Abstract

- **Peppermint prozac.**
  Author(s): Huffington A.
  Source: U.S. News & World Report. 1997 August 18-25; 123(7): 28.
  http://www.ncbi.nlm.nih.gov:80/entrez/query.fcgi?cmd=Retrieve&db=PubMed&list_
  uids=10173120&dopt=Abstract

- **Possible interactions between deprenyl and prozac.**
  Author(s): Suchowersky O, deVries J.
  Source: The Canadian Journal of Neurological Sciences. Le Journal Canadien Des
  Sciences Neurologiques. 1990 August; 17(3): 352-3.
  http://www.ncbi.nlm.nih.gov:80/entrez/query.fcgi?cmd=Retrieve&db=PubMed&list_
  uids=2119870&dopt=Abstract

- **Potential fluoxetine chloride (Prozac) toxicity in a newborn.**
  Author(s): Mhanna MJ, Bennet JB 2nd, Izatt SD.
  Source: Pediatrics. 1997 July; 100(1): 158-9.
  http://www.ncbi.nlm.nih.gov:80/entrez/query.fcgi?cmd=Retrieve&db=PubMed&list_
  uids=9229710&dopt=Abstract

- **Pregnancy outcome following first-trimester exposure to fluoxetine (Prozac)**
  Author(s): Pastuszak A, Schick-Boschetto B, Zuber C, Feldkamp M, Pinelli M, Sihn S,
  Donnenfeld A, McCormack M, Leen-Mitchell M, Woodland C, et al.
  Source: Jama : the Journal of the American Medical Association. 1993 May 5; 269(17):
  2246-8.
  http://www.ncbi.nlm.nih.gov:80/entrez/query.fcgi?cmd=Retrieve&db=PubMed&list_
  uids=8474204&dopt=Abstract

- **Prozac (fluoxetine, Lilly 110140), the first selective serotonin uptake inhibitor and an antidepressant drug: twenty years since its first publication.**
  Author(s): Wong DT, Bymaster FP, Engleman EA.
  Source: Life Sciences. 1995; 57(5): 411-41. Review.
  http://www.ncbi.nlm.nih.gov:80/entrez/query.fcgi?cmd=Retrieve&db=PubMed&list_
  uids=7623609&dopt=Abstract

- **Prozac and suicide.**
  Author(s): Dewan MJ, Masand P.
  Source: The Journal of Family Practice. 1991 September; 33(3): 312.
  http://www.ncbi.nlm.nih.gov:80/entrez/query.fcgi?cmd=Retrieve&db=PubMed&list_uids=1880492&dopt=Abstract

- **Prozac or prilosec for gastric ulcer?**
  Author(s): Costable JM Jr, McKinley MJ.
  Source: The New England Journal of Medicine. 1996 August 22; 335(8): 600.
  http://www.ncbi.nlm.nih.gov:80/entrez/query.fcgi?cmd=Retrieve&db=PubMed&list_uids=8684424&dopt=Abstract

- **Prozac vs. placebos.**
  Author(s): Noonan D, Cowley G.
  Source: Newsweek. 2002 July 15; 140(3): 48-9.
  http://www.ncbi.nlm.nih.gov:80/entrez/query.fcgi?cmd=Retrieve&db=PubMed&list_uids=12150021&dopt=Abstract

- **Prozac weekly.**
  Author(s): Miller MC.
  Source: The Harvard Mental Health Letter / from Harvard Medical School. 2001 July; 18(1): 8.
  http://www.ncbi.nlm.nih.gov:80/entrez/query.fcgi?cmd=Retrieve&db=PubMed&list_uids=11511458&dopt=Abstract

- **Prozac, enhancement, and self-creation.**
  Author(s): DeGrazia D.
  Source: The Hastings Center Report. 2000 March-April; 30(2): 34-40.
  http://www.ncbi.nlm.nih.gov:80/entrez/query.fcgi?cmd=Retrieve&db=PubMed&list_uids=10763472&dopt=Abstract

- **Prozac. A bitter pill.**
  Author(s): McLean B.
  Source: Fortune. 2001 August 13; 144(3): 118-22, 126, 130-2.
  http://www.ncbi.nlm.nih.gov:80/entrez/query.fcgi?cmd=Retrieve&db=PubMed&list_uids=11499050&dopt=Abstract

- **Prozac: panacea or puzzle?**
  Author(s): Stanford SC.
  Source: Trends in Pharmacological Sciences. 1996 April; 17(4): 150-4. Review.
  http://www.ncbi.nlm.nih.gov:80/entrez/query.fcgi?cmd=Retrieve&db=PubMed&list_uids=8984742&dopt=Abstract

- **Prozac: pros and cons.**
  Author(s): Glod C.
  Source: Journal of Psychosocial Nursing and Mental Health Services. 1990 December; 28(12): 33-4.
  http://www.ncbi.nlm.nih.gov:80/entrez/query.fcgi?cmd=Retrieve&db=PubMed&list_uids=2283599&dopt=Abstract

- **Pursued by happiness and beaten senseless. Prozac and the American dream.**
  Author(s): Elliott C.
  Source: The Hastings Center Report. 2000 March-April; 30(2): 7-12.
  http://www.ncbi.nlm.nih.gov:80/entrez/query.fcgi?cmd=Retrieve&db=PubMed&list_uids=10763465&dopt=Abstract

- **The ethics of the broader usage of Prozac: social choice or social bias?**
  Author(s): Weisberger AM.
  Source: Int J Appl Philos. 1995 Summer; 10(1): 69-74. No Abstract Available.
  http://www.ncbi.nlm.nih.gov:80/entrez/query.fcgi?cmd=Retrieve&db=PubMed&list_uids=11902193&dopt=Abstract

- **The perils of Prozac.**
  Author(s): Manolis DC.
  Source: Minn Med. 1995 January; 78(1): 19-23. Review.
  http://www.ncbi.nlm.nih.gov:80/entrez/query.fcgi?cmd=Retrieve&db=PubMed&list_uids=7794331&dopt=Abstract

- **The Prozac children.**
  Author(s): Hampshire M.
  Source: Nurs Times. 1998 January 21-27; 94(3): 12-3. No Abstract Available.
  http://www.ncbi.nlm.nih.gov:80/entrez/query.fcgi?cmd=Retrieve&db=PubMed&list_uids=9510753&dopt=Abstract

- **The use of fluoxetine (Prozac) in premenstrual syndrome: is the incidence of sexual dysfunction and anorgasmia acceptable?**
  Author(s): Olah KS.
  Source: Journal of Obstetrics and Gynaecology : the Journal of the Institute of Obstetrics and Gynaecology. 2002 January; 22(1): 81-3.
  http://www.ncbi.nlm.nih.gov:80/entrez/query.fcgi?cmd=Retrieve&db=PubMed&list_uids=12521737&dopt=Abstract

- **Thinking about Prozac.**
  Author(s): Barondes SH.
  Source: Science. 1994 February 25; 263(5150): 1102-3.
  http://www.ncbi.nlm.nih.gov:80/entrez/query.fcgi?cmd=Retrieve&db=PubMed&list_uids=8108727&dopt=Abstract

- **Tonic clonic seizures and tachycardia induced by fluoxetine (Prozac) overdose.**
  Author(s): Neely JL.
  Source: W V Med J. 1998 September-October; 94(5): 283-5.
  http://www.ncbi.nlm.nih.gov:80/entrez/query.fcgi?cmd=Retrieve&db=PubMed&list_uids=9803888&dopt=Abstract

- **Treatment of fibrositis with fluoxetine hydrochloride (Prozac).**
  Author(s): Geller SA.
  Source: The American Journal of Medicine. 1989 November; 87(5): 594-5.
  http://www.ncbi.nlm.nih.gov:80/entrez/query.fcgi?cmd=Retrieve&db=PubMed&list_uids=2816978&dopt=Abstract

- **Understanding fluoxetine (Prozac).**
  Author(s): Bihm B, Wilson BA.
  Source: Medsurg Nursing : Official Journal of the Academy of Medical-Surgical Nurses.
  1996 February; 5(1): 50-2, 56. Review.
  http://www.ncbi.nlm.nih.gov:80/entrez/query.fcgi?cmd=Retrieve&db=PubMed&list_
  uids=8696409&dopt=Abstract

- **What about Prozac?**
  Author(s): Greenfield DP, Brown JA.
  Source: N J Med. 1992 June; 89(6): 445-6. No Abstract Available.
  http://www.ncbi.nlm.nih.gov:80/entrez/query.fcgi?cmd=Retrieve&db=PubMed&list_
  uids=1620489&dopt=Abstract

- **White paper is linguistic Prozac.**
  Author(s): Nottingham C.
  Source: Nurs Times. 1997 February 26-March 4; 93(9): 23. No Abstract Available.
  http://www.ncbi.nlm.nih.gov:80/entrez/query.fcgi?cmd=Retrieve&db=PubMed&list_
  uids=9095901&dopt=Abstract

- **Your patient and Prozac.**
  Author(s): Matney J.
  Source: Rdh. 1991 March; 11(3): 31-2. No Abstract Available.
  http://www.ncbi.nlm.nih.gov:80/entrez/query.fcgi?cmd=Retrieve&db=PubMed&list_
  uids=1887080&dopt=Abstract

CHAPTER 2. NUTRITION AND PROZAC

Overview

In this chapter, we will show you how to find studies dedicated specifically to nutrition and Prozac.

Finding Nutrition Studies on Prozac

The National Institutes of Health's Office of Dietary Supplements (ODS) offers a searchable bibliographic database called the IBIDS (International Bibliographic Information on Dietary Supplements; National Institutes of Health, Building 31, Room 1B29, 31 Center Drive, MSC 2086, Bethesda, Maryland 20892-2086, Tel: 301-435-2920, Fax: 301-480-1845, E-mail: ods@nih.gov). The IBIDS contains over 460,000 scientific citations and summaries about dietary supplements and nutrition as well as references to published international, scientific literature on dietary supplements such as vitamins, minerals, and botanicals.[7] The IBIDS includes references and citations to both human and animal research studies.

As a service of the ODS, access to the IBIDS database is available free of charge at the following Web address: **http://ods.od.nih.gov/databases/ibids.html.** After entering the search area, you have three choices: (1) IBIDS Consumer Database, (2) Full IBIDS Database, or (3) Peer Reviewed Citations Only.

Now that you have selected a database, click on the "Advanced" tab. An advanced search allows you to retrieve up to 100 fully explained references in a comprehensive format. Type "Prozac" (or synonyms) into the search box, and click "Go." To narrow the search, you can also select the "Title" field.

---

[7] Adapted from **http://ods.od.nih.gov.** IBIDS is produced by the Office of Dietary Supplements (ODS) at the National Institutes of Health to assist the public, healthcare providers, educators, and researchers in locating credible, scientific information on dietary supplements. IBIDS was developed and will be maintained through an interagency partnership with the Food and Nutrition Information Center of the National Agricultural Library, U.S. Department of Agriculture.

The following information is typical of that found when using the "Full IBIDS Database" to search for "Prozac" (or a synonym):

- **From herbal Prozac to Mark McGwire's tonic: how the Dietary Supplement Health and Education Act changed the regulatory landscape for health products.**
  Source: Kaczka, K A J-Contemp-Health-Law-Policy. 2000 Summer; 16(2): 463-99 0882-1046

- **Peppermint prozac.**
  Source: Huffington, A US-News-World-Repage 1997 August 18-25; 123(7): 28 0041-5537

Federal Resources on Nutrition

In addition to the IBIDS, the United States Department of Health and Human Services (HHS) and the United States Department of Agriculture (USDA) provide many sources of information on general nutrition and health. Recommended resources include:

- healthfinder®, HHS's gateway to health information, including diet and nutrition: **http://www.healthfinder.gov/scripts/SearchContext.asp?topic=238&page=0**

- The United States Department of Agriculture's Web site dedicated to nutrition information: **www.nutrition.gov**

- The Food and Drug Administration's Web site for federal food safety information: **www.foodsafety.gov**

- The National Action Plan on Overweight and Obesity sponsored by the United States Surgeon General: **http://www.surgeongeneral.gov/topics/obesity/**

- The Center for Food Safety and Applied Nutrition has an Internet site sponsored by the Food and Drug Administration and the Department of Health and Human Services: **http://vm.cfsan.fda.gov/**

- Center for Nutrition Policy and Promotion sponsored by the United States Department of Agriculture: **http://www.usda.gov/cnpp/**

- Food and Nutrition Information Center, National Agricultural Library sponsored by the United States Department of Agriculture: **http://www.nal.usda.gov/fnic/**

- Food and Nutrition Service sponsored by the United States Department of Agriculture: **http://www.fns.usda.gov/fns/**

Additional Web Resources

A number of additional Web sites offer encyclopedic information covering food and nutrition. The following is a representative sample:

- AOL: **http://search.aol.com/cat.adp?id=174&layer=&from=subcats**

- Family Village: **http://www.familyvillage.wisc.edu/med_nutrition.html**

- Google: **http://directory.google.com/Top/Health/Nutrition/**

- Healthnotes: **http://www.healthnotes.com/**

- Open Directory Project: **http://dmoz.org/Health/Nutrition/**

- Yahoo.com: **http://dir.yahoo.com/Health/Nutrition/**
- WebMD®Health: **http://my.webmd.com/nutrition**
- WholeHealthMD.com: **http://www.wholehealthmd.com/reflib/0,1529,00.html**

CHAPTER 3. ALTERNATIVE MEDICINE AND PROZAC

Overview

In this chapter, we will begin by introducing you to official information sources on complementary and alternative medicine (CAM) relating to Prozac. At the conclusion of this chapter, we will provide additional sources.

National Center for Complementary and Alternative Medicine

The National Center for Complementary and Alternative Medicine (NCCAM) of the National Institutes of Health (http://nccam.nih.gov/) has created a link to the National Library of Medicine's databases to facilitate research for articles that specifically relate to Prozac and complementary medicine. To search the database, go to the following Web site: **http://www.nlm.nih.gov/nccam/camonpubmed.html**. Select "CAM on PubMed." Enter "Prozac" (or synonyms) into the search box. Click "Go." The following references provide information on particular aspects of complementary and alternative medicine that are related to Prozac:

- **A fluoxetine-induced frontal lobe syndrome in an obsessive compulsive patient.**
  Author(s): Hoehn-Saric R, Harris GJ, Pearlson GD, Cox CS, Machlin SR, Camargo EE.
  Source: The Journal of Clinical Psychiatry. 1991 March; 52(3): 131-3.
  http://www.ncbi.nlm.nih.gov:80/entrez/query.fcgi?cmd=Retrieve&db=PubMed&list_uids=2005077&dopt=Abstract

- **A study of the antidepressant activity of Hypericum perforatum on animal models.**
  Author(s): Gambarana C, Tolu PL, Masi F, Rinaldi M, Giachetti D, Morazzoni P, De Montis MG.
  Source: Pharmacopsychiatry. 2001 July; 34 Suppl 1: S42-4.
  http://www.ncbi.nlm.nih.gov:80/entrez/query.fcgi?cmd=Retrieve&db=PubMed&list_uids=11518074&dopt=Abstract

- **Alexithymia in an adolescent with agenesis of the corpus callosum and chronic pain.**
  Author(s): Ernst H, Key JD, Koval MS.

Source: Journal of the American Academy of Child and Adolescent Psychiatry. 1999 October; 38(10): 1212-3.
http://www.ncbi.nlm.nih.gov:80/entrez/query.fcgi?cmd=Retrieve&db=PubMed&list_uids=10517052&dopt=Abstract

- **An East-West approach to the management of central post-stroke pain.**
Author(s): Yen HL, Chan W.
Source: Cerebrovascular Diseases (Basel, Switzerland). 2003; 16(1): 27-30.
http://www.ncbi.nlm.nih.gov:80/entrez/query.fcgi?cmd=Retrieve&db=PubMed&list_uids=12766358&dopt=Abstract

- **Animal behavior case of the month. Periodic aggression toward the owner.**
Author(s): Overall KL.
Source: J Am Vet Med Assoc. 1995 March 1; 206(5): 629-32. No Abstract Available.
http://www.ncbi.nlm.nih.gov:80/entrez/query.fcgi?cmd=Retrieve&db=PubMed&list_uids=7744681&dopt=Abstract

- **Anticonvulsant effect of fluoxetine on focally evoked limbic motor seizures in rats.**
Author(s): Prendiville S, Gale K.
Source: Epilepsia. 1993 March-April; 34(2): 381-4.
http://www.ncbi.nlm.nih.gov:80/entrez/query.fcgi?cmd=Retrieve&db=PubMed&list_uids=8384110&dopt=Abstract

- **Antidepressant activity of aqueous extracts of Curcuma longa in mice.**
Author(s): Yu ZF, Kong LD, Chen Y.
Source: Journal of Ethnopharmacology. 2002 November; 83(1-2): 161-5.
http://www.ncbi.nlm.nih.gov:80/entrez/query.fcgi?cmd=Retrieve&db=PubMed&list_uids=12413724&dopt=Abstract

- **Antidepressant effects of Banxia Houpu decoction, a traditional Chinese medicinal empirical formula.**
Author(s): Luo L, Nong Wang J, Kong LD, Jiang QG, Tan RX.
Source: Journal of Ethnopharmacology. 2000 November; 73(1-2): 277-81.
http://www.ncbi.nlm.nih.gov:80/entrez/query.fcgi?cmd=Retrieve&db=PubMed&list_uids=11025166&dopt=Abstract

- **Ayahuasca preparations and serotonin reuptake inhibitors: a potential combination for severe adverse interactions.**
Author(s): Callaway JC, Grob CS.
Source: J Psychoactive Drugs. 1998 October-December; 30(4): 367-9.
http://www.ncbi.nlm.nih.gov:80/entrez/query.fcgi?cmd=Retrieve&db=PubMed&list_uids=9924842&dopt=Abstract

- **Bitterest pill?**
Author(s): Hampshire M.
Source: Nursing Standard : Official Newspaper of the Royal College of Nursing. 2000 October 11-17; 15(4): 14-5.
http://www.ncbi.nlm.nih.gov:80/entrez/query.fcgi?cmd=Retrieve&db=PubMed&list_uids=11971482&dopt=Abstract

- **Brain function in a patient with torture related post-traumatic stress disorder before and after fluoxetine treatment: a positron emission tomography provocation study.**
  Author(s): Fernandez M, Pissiota A, Frans O, von Knorring L, Fischer H, Fredrikson M.
  Source: Neuroscience Letters. 2001 January 12; 297(2): 101-4.
  http://www.ncbi.nlm.nih.gov:80/entrez/query.fcgi?cmd=Retrieve&db=PubMed&list_uids=11121880&dopt=Abstract

- **Caudate glucose metabolic rate changes with both drug and behavior therapy for obsessive-compulsive disorder.**
  Author(s): Baxter LR Jr, Schwartz JM, Bergman KS, Szuba MP, Guze BH, Mazziotta JC, Alazraki A, Selin CE, Ferng HK, Munford P, et al.
  Source: Archives of General Psychiatry. 1992 September; 49(9): 681-9.
  http://www.ncbi.nlm.nih.gov:80/entrez/query.fcgi?cmd=Retrieve&db=PubMed&list_uids=1514872&dopt=Abstract

- **Cerebral glucose metabolism in childhood-onset obsessive-compulsive disorder. Revisualization during pharmacotherapy.**
  Author(s): Swedo SE, Pietrini P, Leonard HL, Schapiro MB, Rettew DC, Goldberger EL, Rapoport SI, Rapoport JL, Grady CL.
  Source: Archives of General Psychiatry. 1992 September; 49(9): 690-4.
  http://www.ncbi.nlm.nih.gov:80/entrez/query.fcgi?cmd=Retrieve&db=PubMed&list_uids=1514873&dopt=Abstract

- **Clinical characteristics of trichotillomania and its response to fluoxetine.**
  Author(s): Winchel RM, Jones JS, Stanley B, Molcho A, Stanley M.
  Source: The Journal of Clinical Psychiatry. 1992 September; 53(9): 304-8.
  http://www.ncbi.nlm.nih.gov:80/entrez/query.fcgi?cmd=Retrieve&db=PubMed&list_uids=1517191&dopt=Abstract

- **Clinical crossroads: a 45-year-old woman with premenstrual dysphoric disorder.**
  Author(s): Appleton PE.
  Source: Jama : the Journal of the American Medical Association. 1999 June 23-30; 281(24): 2283.
  http://www.ncbi.nlm.nih.gov:80/entrez/query.fcgi?cmd=Retrieve&db=PubMed&list_uids=10386546&dopt=Abstract

- **Comparison of equivalence between the St. John's wort extract LoHyp-57 and fluoxetine.**
  Author(s): Harrer G, Schmidt U, Kuhn U, Biller A.
  Source: Arzneimittel-Forschung. 1999 April; 49(4): 289-96.
  http://www.ncbi.nlm.nih.gov:80/entrez/query.fcgi?cmd=Retrieve&db=PubMed&list_uids=10337446&dopt=Abstract

- **Comparison of hypericum extracts with imipramine and fluoxetine in animal models of depression and alcoholism.**
  Author(s): De Vry J, Maurel S, Schreiber R, de Beun R, Jentzsch KR.

Source: European Neuropsychopharmacology : the Journal of the European College of Neuropsychopharmacology. 1999 December; 9(6): 461-8.
http://www.ncbi.nlm.nih.gov:80/entrez/query.fcgi?cmd=Retrieve&db=PubMed&list_uids=10625112&dopt=Abstract

- **Dichotic listening before and after fluoxetine treatment for major depression: relations of laterality to therapeutic response.**
  Author(s): Bruder GE, Otto MW, McGrath PJ, Stewart JW, Fava M, Rosenbaum JF, Quitkin FM.
  Source: Neuropsychopharmacology : Official Publication of the American College of Neuropsychopharmacology. 1996 August; 15(2): 171-9.
  http://www.ncbi.nlm.nih.gov:80/entrez/query.fcgi?cmd=Retrieve&db=PubMed&list_uids=8840353&dopt=Abstract

- **Differential therapy of mild to moderate depressive episodes (ICD-10 F 32.0; F 32.1) with St. John's wort.**
  Author(s): Friede M, Henneicke von Zepelin HH, Freudenstein J.
  Source: Pharmacopsychiatry. 2001 July; 34 Suppl 1: S38-41.
  http://www.ncbi.nlm.nih.gov:80/entrez/query.fcgi?cmd=Retrieve&db=PubMed&list_uids=11518073&dopt=Abstract

- **Diurnal effects of fluoxetine and naloxone on the human hypothalamic-pituitary-adrenal axis.**
  Author(s): Torpy DJ, Grice JE, Hockings GI, Walters MM, Crosbie GV, Jackson RV.
  Source: Clinical and Experimental Pharmacology & Physiology. 1997 June; 24(6): 421-3.
  http://www.ncbi.nlm.nih.gov:80/entrez/query.fcgi?cmd=Retrieve&db=PubMed&list_uids=9171947&dopt=Abstract

- **Dopamine D2 receptor binding before and after treatment of major depression measured by [123I]IBZM SPECT.**
  Author(s): Klimke A, Larisch R, Janz A, Vosberg H, Muller-Gartner HW, Gaebel W.
  Source: Psychiatry Research. 1999 April 26; 90(2): 91-101.
  http://www.ncbi.nlm.nih.gov:80/entrez/query.fcgi?cmd=Retrieve&db=PubMed&list_uids=10482381&dopt=Abstract

- **Effect of various serotoninergically induced manipulations on audiogenic seizures in magnesium-deficient mice.**
  Author(s): Bac P, Pages N, Herrenknecht C, Dewulf C, Binet P, Durlach J.
  Source: Magnes Res. 1994 June; 7(2): 107-15.
  http://www.ncbi.nlm.nih.gov:80/entrez/query.fcgi?cmd=Retrieve&db=PubMed&list_uids=7999524&dopt=Abstract

- **Effects of 6-methoxy-1,2,3,4-tetrahydro-beta-carboline (6-MeO-THbetaC) on audiogenic seizures in DBA/2J mice.**
  Author(s): Sparks DL, Buckholtz NS.
  Source: Pharmacology, Biochemistry, and Behavior. 1980 January; 12(1): 119-24.
  http://www.ncbi.nlm.nih.gov:80/entrez/query.fcgi?cmd=Retrieve&db=PubMed&list_uids=6768069&dopt=Abstract

- **Effects of fluoxetine on regional cerebral blood flow in obsessive-compulsive patients.**
  Author(s): Hoehn-Saric R, Pearlson GD, Harris GJ, Machlin SR, Camargo EE.
  Source: The American Journal of Psychiatry. 1991 September; 148(9): 1243-5.
  http://www.ncbi.nlm.nih.gov:80/entrez/query.fcgi?cmd=Retrieve&db=PubMed&list_uids=1883007&dopt=Abstract

- **Effects of standardized extracts of St. John's wort on the single-unit activity of serotonergic dorsal Raphe neurons in awake cats: comparisons with fluoxetine and sertraline.**
  Author(s): Fornal CA, Metzler CW, Mirescu C, Stein SK, Jacobs BL.
  Source: Neuropsychopharmacology : Official Publication of the American College of Neuropsychopharmacology. 2001 December; 25(6): 858-70.
  http://www.ncbi.nlm.nih.gov:80/entrez/query.fcgi?cmd=Retrieve&db=PubMed&list_uids=11750179&dopt=Abstract

- **Efficacy and tolerability of Ze 117 St. John's wort extract in comparison with placebo, imipramine and fluoxetine for the treatment of mild to moderate depression according to ICD-10. An overview.**
  Author(s): Kaufeler R, Meier B, Brattstrom A.
  Source: Pharmacopsychiatry. 2001 July; 34 Suppl 1: S49-50. Review.
  http://www.ncbi.nlm.nih.gov:80/entrez/query.fcgi?cmd=Retrieve&db=PubMed&list_uids=11518076&dopt=Abstract

- **Efficacy of an Hypericum perforatum (St. John's wort) extract in preventing and reverting a condition of escape deficit in rats.**
  Author(s): Gambarana C, Ghiglieri O, Tolu P, De Montis MG, Giachetti D, Bombardelli E, Tagliamonte A.
  Source: Neuropsychopharmacology : Official Publication of the American College of Neuropsychopharmacology. 1999 August; 21(2): 247-57.
  http://www.ncbi.nlm.nih.gov:80/entrez/query.fcgi?cmd=Retrieve&db=PubMed&list_uids=10432473&dopt=Abstract

- **Endocrine, neuroendocrine and behavioral effects of oral dehydroepiandrosterone sulfate supplementation in postmenopausal women.**
  Author(s): Stomati M, Rubino S, Spinetti A, Parrini D, Luisi S, Casarosa E, Petraglia F, Genazzani AR.
  Source: Gynecological Endocrinology : the Official Journal of the International Society of Gynecological Endocrinology. 1999 February; 13(1): 15-25.
  http://www.ncbi.nlm.nih.gov:80/entrez/query.fcgi?cmd=Retrieve&db=PubMed&list_uids=10368794&dopt=Abstract

- **Enhancement of the anticonvulsant effect of fluoxetine following blockade of 5-HT1A receptors.**
  Author(s): Browning RA, Wood AV, **Merrill** MA, Dailey JW, Jobe PC.
  Source: European Journal of Pharmacology. 1997 October 1; 336(1): 1-6.
  http://www.ncbi.nlm.nih.gov:80/entrez/query.fcgi?cmd=Retrieve&db=PubMed&list_uids=9384247&dopt=Abstract

- **Equivalence of St John's wort extract (Ze 117) and fluoxetine: a randomized, controlled study in mild-moderate depression.**
  Author(s): Schrader E.
  Source: International Clinical Psychopharmacology. 2000 March; 15(2): 61-8.
  http://www.ncbi.nlm.nih.gov:80/entrez/query.fcgi?cmd=Retrieve&db=PubMed&list_uids=10759336&dopt=Abstract

- **Fluoxetine potentiates nitrazepam-induced behavioral sleep in young chicks.**
  Author(s): Hussaini IM, Musa MH.
  Source: Physiology & Behavior. 1994 February; 55(2): 391-3.
  http://www.ncbi.nlm.nih.gov:80/entrez/query.fcgi?cmd=Retrieve&db=PubMed&list_uids=8153184&dopt=Abstract

- **Fluoxetine versus Vitex agnus castus extract in the treatment of premenstrual dysphoric disorder.**
  Author(s): Atmaca M, Kumru S, Tezcan E.
  Source: Human Psychopharmacology. 2003 April; 18(3): 191-5.
  http://www.ncbi.nlm.nih.gov:80/entrez/query.fcgi?cmd=Retrieve&db=PubMed&list_uids=12672170&dopt=Abstract

- **Fluoxetine-induced genital anesthesia relieved by Ginkgo biloba extract.**
  Author(s): Ellison JM, DeLuca P.
  Source: The Journal of Clinical Psychiatry. 1998 April; 59(4): 199-200.
  http://www.ncbi.nlm.nih.gov:80/entrez/query.fcgi?cmd=Retrieve&db=PubMed&list_uids=9590676&dopt=Abstract

- **From herbal Prozac to Mark McGwire's tonic: how the Dietary Supplement Health and Education Act changed the regulatory landscape for health products.**
  Author(s): Kaczka KA.
  Source: J Contemp Health Law Policy. 2000 Summer; 16(2): 463-99. No Abstract Available.
  http://www.ncbi.nlm.nih.gov:80/entrez/query.fcgi?cmd=Retrieve&db=PubMed&list_uids=10970182&dopt=Abstract

- **Hypericum perforatum versus fluoxetine in the treatment of mild to moderate depression.**
  Author(s): Behnke K, Jensen GS, Graubaum HJ, Gruenwald J.
  Source: Adv Ther. 2002 January-February; 19(1): 43-52.
  http://www.ncbi.nlm.nih.gov:80/entrez/query.fcgi?cmd=Retrieve&db=PubMed&list_uids=12008860&dopt=Abstract

- **Hypomania induced by herbal and pharmaceutical psychotropic medicines following mild traumatic brain injury.**
  Author(s): Spinella M, Eaton LA.
  Source: Brain Injury : [bi]. 2002 April; 16(4): 359-67.
  http://www.ncbi.nlm.nih.gov:80/entrez/query.fcgi?cmd=Retrieve&db=PubMed&list_uids=11953006&dopt=Abstract

- **In vivo visualization of serotonin transporters in the human brain during fluoxetine treatment.**
  Author(s): Tauscher J, Pirker W, de Zwaan M, Asenbaum S, Brucke T, Kasper S.
  Source: European Neuropsychopharmacology : the Journal of the European College of Neuropsychopharmacology. 1999 January; 9(1-2): 177-9.
  http://www.ncbi.nlm.nih.gov:80/entrez/query.fcgi?cmd=Retrieve&db=PubMed&list_uids=10082245&dopt=Abstract

- **Increased plasma concentrations of interleukin-6, soluble interleukin-6, soluble interleukin-2 and transferrin receptor in major depression.**
  Author(s): Maes M, Meltzer HY, Bosmans E, Bergmans R, Vandoolaeghe E, Ranjan R, Desnyder R.
  Source: Journal of Affective Disorders. 1995 August 18; 34(4): 301-9.
  http://www.ncbi.nlm.nih.gov:80/entrez/query.fcgi?cmd=Retrieve&db=PubMed&list_uids=8550956&dopt=Abstract

- **Individual differences in cerebral metabolic patterns during pharmacotherapy in obsessive-compulsive disorder: a multiple regression/discriminant analysis of positron emission tomographic data.**
  Author(s): Azari NP, Pietrini P, Horwitz B, Pettigrew KD, Leonard HL, Rapoport JL, Schapiro MB, Swedo SE.
  Source: Biological Psychiatry. 1993 December 1; 34(11): 798-809.
  http://www.ncbi.nlm.nih.gov:80/entrez/query.fcgi?cmd=Retrieve&db=PubMed&list_uids=8292684&dopt=Abstract

- **Inhibition of vesicular uptake of monoamines by hyperforin.**
  Author(s): Roz N, Mazur Y, Hirshfeld A, Rehavi M.
  Source: Life Sciences. 2002 September 27; 71(19): 2227-37.
  http://www.ncbi.nlm.nih.gov:80/entrez/query.fcgi?cmd=Retrieve&db=PubMed&list_uids=12215370&dopt=Abstract

- **Is St John's wort a 'Prozac-like' herbal antidepressant?**
  Author(s): Gobbi M, Mennini T.
  Source: Trends in Pharmacological Sciences. 2001 November; 22(11): 557-9; Author Reply 559.
  http://www.ncbi.nlm.nih.gov:80/entrez/query.fcgi?cmd=Retrieve&db=PubMed&list_uids=11698096&dopt=Abstract

- **Issues in methodology and applications for therapeutic drug monitoring of fluoxetine and norfluoxetine enantiomers.**
  Author(s): Zuccaro P, Pacifici R, Altieri I, Avenoso A, Pellegrini M, Spina E, Perucca E, Pichini S.
  Source: Therapeutic Drug Monitoring. 1998 February; 20(1): 20-4.
  http://www.ncbi.nlm.nih.gov:80/entrez/query.fcgi?cmd=Retrieve&db=PubMed&list_uids=9485549&dopt=Abstract

- **Mums on Prozac, kids on inhalers: the need for research on the potential for improving health through housing interventions.**
  Author(s): Ellaway A, Macintyre S, Fairley A.

Source: Health Bull (Edinb). 2000 July; 58(4): 336-9.
http://www.ncbi.nlm.nih.gov:80/entrez/query.fcgi?cmd=Retrieve&db=PubMed&list_
uids=12813815&dopt=Abstract

- **Neither intranigral fluoxetine nor 5,7-dihydroxytryptamine alter audiogenic seizures in genetically epilepsy-prone rats.**
  Author(s): Statnick M, Dailey J, Jobe P, Browning R.
  Source: European Journal of Pharmacology. 1996 March 28; 299(1-3): 93-102.
  http://www.ncbi.nlm.nih.gov:80/entrez/query.fcgi?cmd=Retrieve&db=PubMed&list_
  uids=8901011&dopt=Abstract

- **Neurobehavioural dysfunction following mild traumatic brain injury in childhood: a case report with positive findings on positron emission tomography (PET).**
  Author(s): Roberts MA, Manshadi FF, Bushnell DL, Hines ME.
  Source: Brain Injury : [bi]. 1995 July; 9(5): 427-36.
  http://www.ncbi.nlm.nih.gov:80/entrez/query.fcgi?cmd=Retrieve&db=PubMed&list_
  uids=7550214&dopt=Abstract

- **Pathophysiological significance of cerebral perfusion abnormalities in major depression-trait or state marker?**
  Author(s): Bonne O, Krausz Y.
  Source: European Neuropsychopharmacology : the Journal of the European College of Neuropsychopharmacology. 1997 August; 7(3): 225-33.
  http://www.ncbi.nlm.nih.gov:80/entrez/query.fcgi?cmd=Retrieve&db=PubMed&list_
  uids=9213083&dopt=Abstract

- **Pindolol augmentation of antidepressant treatment: recent contributions from brain imaging studies.**
  Author(s): Martinez D, Broft A, Laruelle M.
  Source: Biological Psychiatry. 2000 October 15; 48(8): 844-53. Review.
  http://www.ncbi.nlm.nih.gov:80/entrez/query.fcgi?cmd=Retrieve&db=PubMed&list_
  uids=11063979&dopt=Abstract

- **St John's wort: Prozac from the plant kingdom.**
  Author(s): Di Carlo G, Borrelli F, Ernst E, Izzo AA.
  Source: Trends in Pharmacological Sciences. 2001 June; 22(6): 292-7. Review.
  http://www.ncbi.nlm.nih.gov:80/entrez/query.fcgi?cmd=Retrieve&db=PubMed&list_
  uids=11395157&dopt=Abstract

- **The Prozac boom and its placebogenic counterpart – a culturally fashioned phenomenon.**
  Author(s): Slingsby BT.
  Source: Medical Science Monitor : International Medical Journal of Experimental and Clinical Research. 2002 May; 8(5): Cr389-93.
  http://www.ncbi.nlm.nih.gov:80/entrez/query.fcgi?cmd=Retrieve&db=PubMed&list_
  uids=12016420&dopt=Abstract

Additional Web Resources

A number of additional Web sites offer encyclopedic information covering CAM and related topics. The following is a representative sample:

- Alternative Medicine Foundation, Inc.: **http://www.herbmed.org/**

- AOL: **http://search.aol.com/cat.adp?id=169&layer=&from=subcats**

- Chinese Medicine: **http://www.newcenturynutrition.com/**

- drkoop.com®: **http://www.drkoop.com/InteractiveMedicine/IndexC.html**

- Family Village: **http://www.familyvillage.wisc.edu/med_altn.htm**

- Google: **http://directory.google.com/Top/Health/Alternative/**

- Healthnotes: **http://www.healthnotes.com/**

- MedWebPlus:
  http://medwebplus.com/subject/Alternative_and_Complementary_Medicine

- Open Directory Project: **http://dmoz.org/Health/Alternative/**

- HealthGate: **http://www.tnp.com/**

- WebMD®Health: **http://my.webmd.com/drugs_and_herbs**

- WholeHealthMD.com: **http://www.wholehealthmd.com/reflib/0,1529,00.html**

- Yahoo.com: **http://dir.yahoo.com/Health/Alternative_Medicine/**

The following is a specific Web list relating to Prozac; please note that any particular subject below may indicate either a therapeutic use, or a contraindication (potential danger), and does not reflect an official recommendation:

- **General Overview**

  Anxiety
  Source: Healthnotes, Inc. www.healthnotes.com

  Depression
  Source: Healthnotes, Inc. www.healthnotes.com

  Depression (Mild to Moderate)
  Source: Prima Communications, Inc.www.personalhealthzone.com

  Eating Disorders
  Source: Healthnotes, Inc. www.healthnotes.com

  Fibromyalgia
  Source: Healthnotes, Inc. www.healthnotes.com

  Impotence
  Source: Prima Communications, Inc.www.personalhealthzone.com

Migraine Headaches
Source: Prima Communications, Inc.www.personalhealthzone.com

- **Herbs and Supplements**

5-HTP (5-Hydroxytryptophan)
Source: Prima Communications, Inc.www.personalhealthzone.com

Antidepressants
Source: Healthnotes, Inc. www.healthnotes.com

Fluvoxamine
Source: Healthnotes, Inc. www.healthnotes.com

Ginkgo
Source: Prima Communications, Inc.www.personalhealthzone.com

Phenelzine
Source: Healthnotes, Inc. www.healthnotes.com

Selective Serotonin Reuptake Inhibitors (SSRIs)
Source: Integrative Medicine Communications; www.drkoop.com

St. John's Wort
Source: Prima Communications, Inc.www.personalhealthzone.com

St. John's wort
Source: WholeHealthMD.com, LLC. www.wholehealthmd.com
Hyperlink:
http://www.wholehealthmd.com/refshelf/substances_view/0,1525,824,00.html

Yohimbe
Alternative names: Pausinystalia yohimbe
Source: Healthnotes, Inc. www.healthnotes.com

General References

A good place to find general background information on CAM is the National Library of Medicine. It has prepared within the MEDLINEplus system an information topic page dedicated to complementary and alternative medicine. To access this page, go to the MEDLINEplus site at **http://www.nlm.nih.gov/medlineplus/alternativemedicine.html**. This Web site provides a general overview of various topics and can lead to a number of general sources.

Chapter 4. Dissertations on Prozac

Overview

In this chapter, we will give you a bibliography on recent dissertations relating to Prozac. We will also provide you with information on how to use the Internet to stay current on dissertations. **IMPORTANT NOTE:** When following the search strategy described below, you may discover non-medical dissertations that use the generic term "Prozac" (or a synonym) in their titles. To accurately reflect the results that you might find while conducting research on Prozac, we have not necessarily excluded non-medical dissertations in this bibliography.

Dissertations on Prozac

ProQuest Digital Dissertations, the largest archive of academic dissertations available, is located at the following Web address: **http://wwwlib.umi.com/dissertations**. From this archive, we have compiled the following list covering dissertations devoted to Prozac. You will see that the information provided includes the dissertation's title, its author, and the institution with which the author is associated. The following covers recent dissertations found when using this search procedure:

- **Possession, Purgatives or Prozac? the Experience of Illness and the Process of Healing in Kerala, South India** by Halliburton, Murphy John; Phd from City University of New York, 2000, 319 pages
  http://wwwlib.umi.com/dissertations/fullcit/9969693

- **The Freud of Prozac: Tracing Psychotropic Medications Through American Culture, 1955--2001** by Metzl, Jonathan Michel; Phd from University of Michigan, 2001, 293 pages
  http://wwwlib.umi.com/dissertations/fullcit/3001011

- **Utilizing Fluoxetine Hydrochloride and Cognitive Therapy in the Treatment of Chronic Situational Depression among Women (prozac)** by Scheetz, Vicki Lee, Phd from The Ohio State University, 1994, 112 pages
  http://wwwlib.umi.com/dissertations/fullcit/9427783

Keeping Current

Ask the medical librarian at your library if it has full and unlimited access to the *ProQuest Digital Dissertations* database. From the library, you should be able to do more complete searches via **http://wwwlib.umi.com/dissertations**.

CHAPTER 5. CLINICAL TRIALS AND PROZAC

Overview

In this chapter, we will show you how to keep informed of the latest clinical trials concerning Prozac.

Recent Trials on Prozac

The following is a list of recent trials dedicated to Prozac.[8] Further information on a trial is available at the Web site indicated.

- **Effect of Fluoxetine (Prozac) on Domestic Violence**

  Condition(s): Domestic Violence

  Study Status: This study is currently recruiting patients.

  Sponsor(s): National Institute on Alcohol Abuse and Alcoholism (NIAAA)

  Purpose - Excerpt: This study will evaluate whether fluoxetine (Prozac), used together with traditional psychotherapy, can reduce aggression in people who are physically violent towards their spouses or significant others. Treatment for domestic violence has centered on behavioral therapies, such as anger management and self-control exercises. Recent studies have shown that fluoxetine-a drug commonly used to treat depression and panic disorder-can decrease acts of aggression. Men and women between the ages of 18 and 65 who have a history of inflicting physical aggression on a spouses or significant others in the past year (with at least one episode occurring not under the influence of alcohol) may be eligible for this study. Participants spouses or significant others will also be asked to participate. All potential participants will be screened with a medical and psychiatric evaluation and history, breath alcohol analysis, blood tests, urine drug screen and electrocardiogram Those enrolled will undergo the following procedures: Perpetrator -Interview and questionnaires - Participants will be interviewed by a social worker about past and current mental health and use of alcohol and illicit drugs and will complete questionnaires assessing emotional state and personality, depression, anxiety, aggression and alcohol consumption. Some of the questionnaires will be repeated at monthly intervals. -Physical performance testing - Performance and

---

[8] These are listed at **www.ClinicalTrials.gov**.

speed will be measured in three separate training sessions that involve repeatedly pressing a button on a button box console, earning points worth money. -Dyadic interaction paradigm - Participants will interact with their spouse/significant other in a small room, first discussing a neutral topic, such as the day's events, and then a subject that has been a source of conflict. -Fluoxetine administration - Participants will be randomly assigned to receive either 10 mg. of fluoxetine or placebo (identical capsules with no active ingredients) once a day for 3 days, then twice a day, increasing up to four capsules a day if there are no serious side effects. Blood will be drawn once a month to measure drug levels. At the end of 3 months, participants taking placebo may remain in the study and receive fluoxetine. -Clinic visits - Participants are followed in the clinic weekly for the first month, then twice a month for the next 2 months for adjustment of number of pills, evaluation of aggressive behavior and alcohol consumption, and therapy for issues of self-esteem, anger management and communication skills. Couples therapy aimed at conflict resolution and improving communication skills will be offered. -Genetic tests (optional) - Blood will be drawn to determine if there is a relationship between genes involved in a chemical process (serotonin reuptake) that is influenced by fluoxetine and the participant's response to the drug. Spouse/Significant other: Spouses/significant others will complete several questionnaires once a month (total 4 times) to rate their partners' behavior while in the study. They will also participate in the dyadic interaction paradigm described above at the beginning and end of the study.

Phase(s): Phase II; MEDLINEplus consumer health information

Study Type: Interventional

Contact(s): see Web site below

Web Site: http://clinicaltrials.gov/ct/show/NCT00011765

Keeping Current on Clinical Trials

The U.S. National Institutes of Health, through the National Library of Medicine, has developed ClinicalTrials.gov to provide current information about clinical research across the broadest number of diseases and conditions.

The site was launched in February 2000 and currently contains approximately 5,700 clinical studies in over 59,000 locations worldwide, with most studies being conducted in the United States. ClinicalTrials.gov receives about 2 million hits per month and hosts approximately 5,400 visitors daily. To access this database, simply go to the Web site at **http://www.clinicaltrials.gov/** and search by "Prozac" (or synonyms).

While ClinicalTrials.gov is the most comprehensive listing of NIH-supported clinical trials available, not all trials are in the database. The database is updated regularly, so clinical trials are continually being added. The following is a list of specialty databases affiliated with the National Institutes of Health that offer additional information on trials:

- For clinical studies at the Warren Grant Magnuson Clinical Center located in Bethesda, Maryland, visit their Web site: **http://clinicalstudies.info.nih.gov/**

- For clinical studies conducted at the Bayview Campus in Baltimore, Maryland, visit their Web site: **http://www.jhbmc.jhu.edu/studies/index.html**

- For cancer trials, visit the National Cancer Institute: **http://cancertrials.nci.nih.gov/**

- For eye-related trials, visit and search the Web page of the National Eye Institute: **http://www.nei.nih.gov/neitrials/index.htm**

- For heart, lung and blood trials, visit the Web page of the National Heart, Lung and Blood Institute: **http://www.nhlbi.nih.gov/studies/index.htm**

- For trials on aging, visit and search the Web site of the National Institute on Aging: **http://www.grc.nia.nih.gov/studies/index.htm**

- For rare diseases, visit and search the Web site sponsored by the Office of Rare Diseases: **http://ord.aspensys.com/asp/resources/rsch_trials.asp**

- For alcoholism, visit the National Institute on Alcohol Abuse and Alcoholism: **http://www.niaaa.nih.gov/intramural/Web_dicbr_hp/particip.htm**

- For trials on infectious, immune, and allergic diseases, visit the site of the National Institute of Allergy and Infectious Diseases: **http://www.niaid.nih.gov/clintrials/**

- For trials on arthritis, musculoskeletal and skin diseases, visit newly revised site of the National Institute of Arthritis and Musculoskeletal and Skin Diseases of the National Institutes of Health: **http://www.niams.nih.gov/hi/studies/index.htm**

- For hearing-related trials, visit the National Institute on Deafness and Other Communication Disorders: **http://www.nidcd.nih.gov/health/clinical/index.htm**

- For trials on diseases of the digestive system and kidneys, and diabetes, visit the National Institute of Diabetes and Digestive and Kidney Diseases: **http://www.niddk.nih.gov/patient/patient.htm**

- For drug abuse trials, visit and search the Web site sponsored by the National Institute on Drug Abuse: **http://www.nida.nih.gov/CTN/Index.htm**

- For trials on mental disorders, visit and search the Web site of the National Institute of Mental Health: **http://www.nimh.nih.gov/studies/index.cfm**

- For trials on neurological disorders and stroke, visit and search the Web site sponsored by the National Institute of Neurological Disorders and Stroke of the NIH: **http://www.ninds.nih.gov/funding/funding_opportunities.htm#Clinical_Trials**

CHAPTER 6. BOOKS ON PROZAC

Overview

This chapter provides bibliographic book references relating to Prozac. In addition to online booksellers such as **www.amazon.com** and **www.bn.com**, excellent sources for book titles on Prozac include the Combined Health Information Database and the National Library of Medicine. Your local medical library also may have these titles available for loan.

Book Summaries: Online Booksellers

Commercial Internet-based booksellers, such as Amazon.com and Barnes&Noble.com, offer summaries which have been supplied by each title's publisher. Some summaries also include customer reviews. Your local bookseller may have access to in-house and commercial databases that index all published books (e.g. Books in Print®). **IMPORTANT NOTE:** Online booksellers typically produce search results for medical and non-medical books. When searching for "Prozac" at online booksellers' Web sites, you may discover <u>non-medical books</u> that use the generic term "Prozac" (or a synonym) in their titles. The following is indicative of the results you might find when searching for "Prozac" (sorted alphabetically by title; follow the hyperlink to view more details at Amazon.com):

- **5-HTP The Natural Alternative to Prozac** by John Morgenthaler, Lane Lenard; ISBN: 0962741841;
  http://www.amazon.com/exec/obidos/ASIN/0962741841/icongroupinterna

- **A History of Psychiatry : From the Era of the Asylum to the Age of Prozac** by Edward Shorter (Author) (1998); ISBN: 0471245313;
  http://www.amazon.com/exec/obidos/ASIN/0471245313/icongroupinterna

- **Autumn Ashes: From Presley to Prozac** by Salvatore Marascia (2001); ISBN: 0738868116;
  http://www.amazon.com/exec/obidos/ASIN/0738868116/icongroupinterna

- **Barking at Prozac: My Diary** by Tom McNichol, Merle Nacht (Illustrator) (1996); ISBN: 0517886650;
  http://www.amazon.com/exec/obidos/ASIN/0517886650/icongroupinterna

- **Better living : in pursuit of happiness from Plato to prozac** by Mark Kingwell; ISBN: 0670875023;
  http://www.amazon.com/exec/obidos/ASIN/0670875023/icongroupinterna

- **Better Than Prozac: Creating the Next Generation of Psychiatric Drugs** by Samuel H. Barondes (2003); ISBN: 0195151305;
  http://www.amazon.com/exec/obidos/ASIN/0195151305/icongroupinterna

- **Beyond Prozac : Antidotes for Modern Times** by Michael J. Norden (Author) (1996); ISBN: 0060987073;
  http://www.amazon.com/exec/obidos/ASIN/0060987073/icongroupinterna

- **Beyond Prozac: Healing Mental Suffering Without Drugs** by Terry Lynch (2001); ISBN: 1860231365;
  http://www.amazon.com/exec/obidos/ASIN/1860231365/icongroupinterna

- **Cooking With Prozac: From Nuts to Soup** by Robin Cohn, Richard Courtney (Editor); ISBN: 1886371075;
  http://www.amazon.com/exec/obidos/ASIN/1886371075/icongroupinterna

- **Everything You Need to Know About Prozac** by Jeffrey M. Jonas, et al (1991); ISBN: 0553291920;
  http://www.amazon.com/exec/obidos/ASIN/0553291920/icongroupinterna

- **From the back row : a list of veterinary school stresses as viewed by a student on Prozac** by Dean Scott; ISBN: 0964151820;
  http://www.amazon.com/exec/obidos/ASIN/0964151820/icongroupinterna

- **In Pursuit of Happiness : Better Living from Plato to Prozac** by Mark Kingwell; ISBN: 0609605356;
  http://www.amazon.com/exec/obidos/ASIN/0609605356/icongroupinterna

- **Just How Smart is Prozac?** by Makram K. Girgis (1995); ISBN: 0875275176;
  http://www.amazon.com/exec/obidos/ASIN/0875275176/icongroupinterna

- **Listening to Prozac** by Peter D. Kramer (1997); ISBN: 0140266712;
  http://www.amazon.com/exec/obidos/ASIN/0140266712/icongroupinterna

- **Listening to Prozac/a Psychiatrist Explores Antidepressant Drugs and the Remaking of the Self** by Peter D. Kramer; ISBN: 0670841838;
  http://www.amazon.com/exec/obidos/ASIN/0670841838/icongroupinterna

- **Living With Prozac: And Other Seratonin-Reuptake Inhibitors** by Debra Elfenbein (Editor), Peter Kramer; ISBN: 0062512064;
  http://www.amazon.com/exec/obidos/ASIN/0062512064/icongroupinterna

- **Making the Prozac Decision: Your Guide to Antidepressants** by Carol Ann Turkington, Eliot F. Kaplan; ISBN: 1565651537;
  http://www.amazon.com/exec/obidos/ASIN/1565651537/icongroupinterna

- **Natural Prozac : Learning to Release Your Body's Own Anti-Depressants** by Joel C. Robertson (Author) (1998); ISBN: 0062513540;
  http://www.amazon.com/exec/obidos/ASIN/0062513540/icongroupinterna

- **Nature's Prozac: Natural Therapies and Techniques to Rid Yourself of Anxiety, Depression, Panic Attacks & Stress** by Judith Sachs, Lendon H. Smith; ISBN: 0138876541;
  http://www.amazon.com/exec/obidos/ASIN/0138876541/icongroupinterna

- **Nature's Prozac: Natural Ways to Achieve Peak Health** by Judith Sachs; ISBN: 0671029576;
  http://www.amazon.com/exec/obidos/ASIN/0671029576/icongroupinterna

- **Pharmaceutical Nation: An Obsessive Study of Pill Marketing, Art, History and Culture from Flinstones Vitamins to Prozac (Citadel Underground Series)** by Jim Hogshire; ISBN: 0806517913;
  http://www.amazon.com/exec/obidos/ASIN/0806517913/icongroupinterna

- **Plato, Not Prozac!: Applying Eternal Wisdom to Everyday Problems** by Lou Marinoff (Author) (2000); ISBN: 0060931361;
  http://www.amazon.com/exec/obidos/ASIN/0060931361/icongroupinterna

- **Potatoes Not Prozac: A Natural Seven-step Dietary Plan to Control Depression, Food Cravings and Weight Gain** by Kathleen DesMaisons; ISBN: 0684851490;
  http://www.amazon.com/exec/obidos/ASIN/0684851490/icongroupinterna

- **Potatoes Not Prozac: How to Control Depression, Food Cravings and Weight Gain** by Kathleen Demaisons; ISBN: 0671773771;
  http://www.amazon.com/exec/obidos/ASIN/0671773771/icongroupinterna

- **Prozac (Fluoxetine -Side Effects & Harmful Reaction: Index of New Information with Authors and Subject)** by American Health Research Institute; ISBN: 078830173X;
  http://www.amazon.com/exec/obidos/ASIN/078830173X/icongroupinterna

- **Prozac and Other Antidepressants (Junior Drug Awareness)** by Stephen Bird, et al; ISBN: 0791052044;
  http://www.amazon.com/exec/obidos/ASIN/0791052044/icongroupinterna

- **Prozac and Other Psychiatric Drugs** by Lewis A. Opler, Carol Bialkowski (Contributor) (1996); ISBN: 0671510703;
  http://www.amazon.com/exec/obidos/ASIN/0671510703/icongroupinterna

- **Prozac and Prosperity: Living in the Land of Oz** by Robert Salata (2001); ISBN: 0759625247;
  http://www.amazon.com/exec/obidos/ASIN/0759625247/icongroupinterna

- **Prozac and the New Antidepressants: What You Need to Know About Prozac, Zoloft, Paxil, Luvox, Wellbutrin, Effexor, Serzone, and More** by William S. Appleton (1997); ISBN: 0452274435;
  http://www.amazon.com/exec/obidos/ASIN/0452274435/icongroupinterna

- **Prozac and the New Antidepressants: What You Need to Know About Prozac, Zoloft, Paxil, Luvox, Wellbutrin, Effexor, Serzone, Vestra, Celexa, St. John's Wort, and Others** by William S. Appleton (2000); ISBN: 0452281644;
  http://www.amazon.com/exec/obidos/ASIN/0452281644/icongroupinterna

- **Prozac Backlash: Overcoming the Dangers of Prozac, Zoloft, Paxil, and Other Antidepressants with Safe, Effective Alternatives** by Joseph Glenmullen (Author) (2001); ISBN: 0743200624;
  http://www.amazon.com/exec/obidos/ASIN/0743200624/icongroupinterna

- **Prozac Diary** by Lauren Slater (1999); ISBN: 0140263942;
  http://www.amazon.com/exec/obidos/ASIN/0140263942/icongroupinterna

- **Prozac Highway** by Persimmon Blackbridge; ISBN: 071453059X;
  http://www.amazon.com/exec/obidos/ASIN/071453059X/icongroupinterna

- **Prozac Nation: Young and Depressed in America: A Memoir** by Elizabeth Wurtzel (1997); ISBN: 1573225126;
http://www.amazon.com/exec/obidos/ASIN/1573225126/icongroupinterna

- **Prozac on the Couch: Prescribing Gender in the Era of Wonder Drugs** by Jonathan Michel Metzl (2003); ISBN: 082233061X;
http://www.amazon.com/exec/obidos/ASIN/082233061X/icongroupinterna

- **Prozac Poet** by Vickie Gordon (Editor), et al; ISBN: 1891601024;
http://www.amazon.com/exec/obidos/ASIN/1891601024/icongroupinterna

- **Prozac: Panacea or Pandora? the Rest of the Story on the New Class of Ssri Antidepressants Prozac, Zoloft, Paxil, Lovan, Luvox & More.** by Chase Shephard (Illustrator), et al (1994); ISBN: 0916095592;
http://www.amazon.com/exec/obidos/ASIN/0916095592/icongroupinterna

- **Prozac: Pros & Cons** by Jim Parker (1996); ISBN: 0892302453;
http://www.amazon.com/exec/obidos/ASIN/0892302453/icongroupinterna

- **Prozac: Questions and Answers for Patients, Family and Physicians** by Ronald R. Fieve (Author); ISBN: 0380777185;
http://www.amazon.com/exec/obidos/ASIN/0380777185/icongroupinterna

- **Prozac: The Controversial Cure (Drug Abuse Prevention)** by Helen C. Packard; ISBN: 082392551X;
http://www.amazon.com/exec/obidos/ASIN/082392551X/icongroupinterna

- **Prozac-Free** by Judyth Reichenberg-Ullman, et al; ISBN: 1556433921;
http://www.amazon.com/exec/obidos/ASIN/1556433921/icongroupinterna

- **Prozac-Free: Homeopathic Medicine for Depression, Anxiety, and Other Mental and Emotional Problems** by Judyth Reichenberg-Ullman, Robert Ullman; ISBN: 0761514783;
http://www.amazon.com/exec/obidos/ASIN/0761514783/icongroupinterna

- **Psychobiological Research: Prozac, Schizophrenia & Depression in the Elderly** by Carlos A. Bonilla; ISBN: 1879774062;
http://www.amazon.com/exec/obidos/ASIN/1879774062/icongroupinterna

- **Scorpio Men on Prozac** by Rand Marsh; ISBN: 0738822108;
http://www.amazon.com/exec/obidos/ASIN/0738822108/icongroupinterna

- **Talking Back to Prozac: What Doctors Won't Tell You About Today's Most Controversial Drug** by Peter R. Breggin, Ginger Ross Breggin (Contributor); ISBN: 0312956061;
http://www.amazon.com/exec/obidos/ASIN/0312956061/icongroupinterna

- **The Anti-Depressant Fact Book: What Your Doctor Won't Tell You About Prozac, Zoloft, Paxil, Celexa, and Luvox** by Peter R. Breggin, M.D. Peter R. Breggin; ISBN: 073820451X;
http://www.amazon.com/exec/obidos/ASIN/073820451X/icongroupinterna

- **The Natural Prozac Program: How to Use St. John's Wort, the Antidepressant Herb** by Jonathan Zuess; ISBN: 060980152X;
http://www.amazon.com/exec/obidos/ASIN/060980152X/icongroupinterna

- **The Prozac Alternative: Natural Relief from Depression With St. John's Wort, Kava, Ginkgo, 5-Htp, Homeopathy, and Other Alternative Therapies** by Ran Knishinsky (1998); ISBN: 0892817917;
http://www.amazon.com/exec/obidos/ASIN/0892817917/icongroupinterna

- **The Prozac Conspiracy: A Novel Exposing the Mass-Production of Mental Illness** by David Seymour (2001); ISBN: 075964814X; http://www.amazon.com/exec/obidos/ASIN/075964814X/icongroupinterna

- **The Shooting Drugs - Prozac and its Generation Exposed on the Internet** by Donna Smart; ISBN: 0967307635; http://www.amazon.com/exec/obidos/ASIN/0967307635/icongroupinterna

- **Why Kids Don't Have Heart Attacks: 7 Reasons Kids Have Fun While Adults Have Prozac** by Julius Henderson; ISBN: 0971455600; http://www.amazon.com/exec/obidos/ASIN/0971455600/icongroupinterna

- **Zoloft, Paxil, Luvox and Prozac: All New Information to Help You Choose the Right Antidepressant** by Donald L. Sullivan, Craig Williams (Introduction); ISBN: 0380795183; http://www.amazon.com/exec/obidos/ASIN/0380795183/icongroupinterna

The National Library of Medicine Book Index

The National Library of Medicine at the National Institutes of Health has a massive database of books published on healthcare and biomedicine. Go to the following Internet site, **http://locatorplus.gov/**, and then select "Search LOCATORplus." Once you are in the search area, simply type "Prozac" (or synonyms) into the search box, and select "books only." From there, results can be sorted by publication date, author, or relevance. The following was recently catalogued by the National Library of Medicine:[9]

- **A history of psychiatry: from the era of the asylum to the age of Prozac** Author: Shorter, Edward.; Year: 1997; New York: John Wiley; Sons, c1997; ISBN: 047115749X http://www.amazon.com/exec/obidos/ASIN/047115749X/icongroupinterna

- **Beyond Prozac: brain-toxic lifestyles, natural antidotes & new generation antidepressants** Author: Norden, Michael J.,; Year: 1995; New York: ReganBooks, c1995; ISBN: 0060391510 http://www.amazon.com/exec/obidos/ASIN/0060391510/icongroupinterna

- **The Freud of Prozac: tracing psychotropic medications through American culture, 1955-2001** Author: Metzl, Jonathan,; Year: 2001; 2001

Chapters on Prozac

In order to find chapters that specifically relate to Prozac, an excellent source of abstracts is the Combined Health Information Database. You will need to limit your search to book chapters and Prozac using the "Detailed Search" option. Go to the following hyperlink: **http://chid.nih.gov/detail/detail.html**. To find book chapters, use the drop boxes at the bottom of the search page where "You may refine your search by." Select the dates and

---

[9] In addition to LOCATORPlus, in collaboration with authors and publishers, the National Center for Biotechnology Information (NCBI) is currently adapting biomedical books for the Web. The books may be accessed in two ways: (1) by searching directly using any search term or phrase (in the same way as the bibliographic database PubMed), or (2) by following the links to PubMed abstracts. Each PubMed abstract has a "Books" button that displays a facsimile of the abstract in which some phrases are hypertext links. These phrases are also found in the books available at NCBI. Click on hyperlinked results in the list of books in which the phrase is found. Currently, the majority of the links are between the books and PubMed. In the future, more links will be created between the books and other types of information, such as gene and protein sequences and macromolecular structures. See **http://www.ncbi.nlm.nih.gov/entrez/query.fcgi?db=Books**.

language you prefer, and the format option "Book Chapter." Type "Prozac" (or synonyms) into the "For these words:" box.

CHAPTER 7. MULTIMEDIA ON PROZAC

Overview

In this chapter, we show you how to keep current on multimedia sources of information on Prozac. We start with sources that have been summarized by federal agencies, and then show you how to find bibliographic information catalogued by the National Library of Medicine.

Bibliography: Multimedia on Prozac

The National Library of Medicine is a rich source of information on healthcare-related multimedia productions including slides, computer software, and databases. To access the multimedia database, go to the following Web site: **http://locatorplus.gov/**. Select "Search LOCATORplus." Once in the search area, simply type in Prozac (or synonyms). Then, in the option box provided below the search box, select "Audiovisuals and Computer Files." From there, you can choose to sort results by publication date, author, or relevance. The following multimedia has been indexed on Prozac (for more information, follow the hyperlink indicated):

- **Prozac diary [videorecording]** Source: a presentation of Films for the Humanities & Sciences, BBC Education & Training; Year: 1997; Format: Videorecording; Princeton, N.J.: Films for the Humanities & Sciences, c1997

- **What about prozac [videorecording]** Source: Ambrose Video Publishing, Inc; Year: 1991; Format: Videorecording; New York, N.Y.: CBS; New York: Ambrose Video Publishing, c1991

CHAPTER 8. PERIODICALS AND NEWS ON PROZAC

Overview

In this chapter, we suggest a number of news sources and present various periodicals that cover Prozac.

News Services and Press Releases

One of the simplest ways of tracking press releases on Prozac is to search the news wires. In the following sample of sources, we will briefly describe how to access each service. These services only post recent news intended for public viewing.

PR Newswire

To access the PR Newswire archive, simply go to **http://www.prnewswire.com/**. Select your country. Type "Prozac" (or synonyms) into the search box. You will automatically receive information on relevant news releases posted within the last 30 days. The search results are shown by order of relevance.

Reuters Health

The Reuters' Medical News and Health eLine databases can be very useful in exploring news archives relating to Prozac. While some of the listed articles are free to view, others are available for purchase for a nominal fee. To access this archive, go to **http://www.reutershealth.com/en/index.html** and search by "Prozac" (or synonyms). The following was recently listed in this archive for Prozac:

- **Dr. Reddy's net falls on lower Prozac sales, costs**
  Source: Reuters Industry Breifing
  Date: July 31, 2003
  http://www.reutershealth.com/archive/2003/07/31/business/links/20030731inds003.html

- **Prozac kills lymphoma cancer cells -- scientists**
  Source: Reuters Industry Breifing
  Date: April 15, 2003

- **Prozac kills Burkitt's lymphoma cells: scientists**
  Source: Reuters Health eLine
  Date: April 15, 2003

- **Italian pediatricians back Prozac for children**
  Source: Reuters Industry Breifing
  Date: January 20, 2003

- **Italian doctors back Prozac for kids**
  Source: Reuters Health eLine
  Date: January 20, 2003

- **FDA approves Prozac for pediatric population**
  Source: Reuters Industry Breifing
  Date: January 03, 2003

- **FDA approves Prozac for pediatric depression and OCD**
  Source: Reuters Medical News
  Date: January 03, 2003

- **FDA approves Prozac for children, teens**
  Source: Reuters Health eLine
  Date: January 03, 2003

- **Galen gets boost from pre-menstrual Prozac**
  Source: Reuters Industry Breifing
  Date: December 09, 2002

- **Dr. Reddy's Q2 net drops 31% on Prozac woes**
  Source: Reuters Industry Breifing
  Date: October 24, 2002

- **FDA clears Morton Grove's generic liquid Prozac**
  Source: Reuters Industry Breifing
  Date: September 05, 2002

- **Lilly's Prozac cleared for panic disorder, long-term bulimia treatment**
  Source: Reuters Industry Breifing
  Date: August 15, 2002

- **Lilly settles case over Prozac e-mail**
  Source: Reuters Industry Breifing
  Date: July 26, 2002

- **Drugmaker settles case over Prozac e-mail**
  Source: Reuters Health eLine
  Date: July 26, 2002

- **Florida probes Prozac mailings**
  Source: Reuters Health eLine
  Date: July 09, 2002

- **Florida AG probes Prozac mailings**
  Source: Reuters Industry Breifing
  Date: July 08, 2002

- **Hi-Tech joins list of drugmakers selling Prozac generic**
  Source: Reuters Industry Breifing
  Date: July 01, 2002

- **FTC finalizes privacy settlement with Prozac maker**
  Source: Reuters Health eLine
  Date: May 13, 2002

- **FTC finalizes Lilly Prozac privacy violation settlement**
  Source: Reuters Industry Breifing
  Date: May 13, 2002

- **Prozac may help those with body image disorder**
  Source: Reuters Health eLine
  Date: April 17, 2002

- **Prozac may offer short-term fibromyalgia relief**
  Source: Reuters Health eLine
  Date: March 21, 2002

- **Biological basis of Prozac's effects explored**
  Source: Reuters Health eLine
  Date: March 04, 2002

- **Ivax approved to sell generic Prozac**
  Source: Reuters Industry Breifing
  Date: February 01, 2002

- **Watson gets FDA approval for generic Prozac**
  Source: Reuters Industry Breifing
  Date: January 29, 2002

- **Dr Reddy's Q3 net soars on Prozac generic**
  Source: Reuters Industry Breifing
  Date: January 29, 2002

- **Barr's Q2 profits up on strong generic Prozac, tamoxifen sales**
  Source: Reuters Industry Breifing
  Date: January 29, 2002

- **FTC confirms Lilly settlement for Prozac privacy violation**
  Source: Reuters Industry Breifing
  Date: January 18, 2002

- **Supreme Court rejects Lilly's Prozac patent appeal**
  Source: Reuters Industry Breifing
  Date: January 14, 2002

- **Barr says gets full 180 days with generic Prozac**
  Source: Reuters Industry Breifing
  Date: January 09, 2002

The NIH

Within MEDLINEplus, the NIH has made an agreement with the New York Times Syndicate, the AP News Service, and Reuters to deliver news that can be browsed by the public. Search news releases at **http://www.nlm.nih.gov/medlineplus/alphanews_a.html**. MEDLINEplus allows you to browse across an alphabetical index. Or you can search by date at the following Web page: **http://www.nlm.nih.gov/medlineplus/newsbydate.html**. Often, news items are indexed by MEDLINEplus within its search engine.

Business Wire

Business Wire is similar to PR Newswire. To access this archive, simply go to **http://www.businesswire.com/**. You can scan the news by industry category or company name.

Market Wire

Market Wire is more focused on technology than the other wires. To browse the latest press releases by topic, such as alternative medicine, biotechnology, fitness, healthcare, legal, nutrition, and pharmaceuticals, access Market Wire's Medical/Health channel at **http://www.marketwire.com/mw/release_index?channel=MedicalHealth**. Or simply go to Market Wire's home page at **http://www.marketwire.com/mw/home**, type "Prozac" (or synonyms) into the search box, and click on "Search News." As this service is technology oriented, you may wish to use it when searching for press releases covering diagnostic procedures or tests.

Search Engines

Medical news is also available in the news sections of commercial Internet search engines. See the health news page at Yahoo (**http://dir.yahoo.com/Health/News_and_Media/**), or you can use this Web site's general news search page at **http://news.yahoo.com/**. Type in "Prozac" (or synonyms). If you know the name of a company that is relevant to Prozac, you can go to any stock trading Web site (such as **http://www.etrade.com/**) and search for the company name there. News items across various news sources are reported on indicated hyperlinks. Google offers a similar service at **http://news.google.com/**.

BBC

Covering news from a more European perspective, the British Broadcasting Corporation (BBC) allows the public free access to their news archive located at **http://www.bbc.co.uk/**. Search by "Prozac" (or synonyms).

Newsletter Articles

Use the Combined Health Information Database, and limit your search criteria to "newsletter articles." Again, you will need to use the "Detailed Search" option. Go directly to the following hyperlink: **http://chid.nih.gov/detail/detail.html** Go to the bottom of the search page where "You may refine your search by." Select the dates and language that you prefer. For the format option, select "Newsletter Article." Type "Prozac" (or synonyms) into the "For these words:" box. You should check back periodically with this database as it is updated every three months. The following is a typical result when searching for newsletter articles on Prozac:

- **PXE and Depression**

  Source: PXE Awareness. 9(3): 8-11. 2002.

  Contact: Available from National Association for Pseudoxanthoma Elasticum (NAPE, Inc.). 3500 East 12th Avenue, Denver, CO 80206. (303) 355-3866. Fax (303) 355-3859. E-mail: pxenape@estreet.com. Website: www.napxe.org.

  Summary: This newsletter article provides people who have pseudoxanthoma elasticum (PXE) with information on depression. Some of the more common symptoms of depression, such as sadness, tears, and hopelessness, may not be present in people who have PXE. Instead, lethargy, loss of interest in activities, inability to concentrate, memory impairment, and impaired ability to care for one's self are more prevalent. Heredity may be a factor in the transmission of depression. The severity of a person's illness may not necessarily predict the presence or seriousness of depression. The article lists the symptoms for major depression as provided by the Diagnostic and Statistical Manual of Mental Disorders, Fourth Edition, of the American Psychiatric Association. Five or more of the symptoms must be present during the same two week period to meet the diagnostic criteria of major depression. In addition, the article discusses the treatments that are available, including antidepressants such as **prozac,** cognitive behavioral therapy, and interpersonal therapy.

Academic Periodicals covering Prozac

Numerous periodicals are currently indexed within the National Library of Medicine's PubMed database that are known to publish articles relating to Prozac. In addition to these sources, you can search for articles covering Prozac that have been published by any of the periodicals listed in previous chapters. To find the latest studies published, go to **http://www.ncbi.nlm.nih.gov/pubmed**, type the name of the periodical into the search box, and click "Go."

If you want complete details about the historical contents of a journal, you can also visit the following Web site: **http://www.ncbi.nlm.nih.gov/entrez/jrbrowser.cgi**. Here, type in the name of the journal or its abbreviation, and you will receive an index of published articles. At **http://locatorplus.gov/**, you can retrieve more indexing information on medical periodicals (e.g. the name of the publisher). Select the button "Search LOCATORplus." Then type in the name of the journal and select the advanced search option "Journal Title Search."

APPENDICES

APPENDIX A. PHYSICIAN RESOURCES

Overview

In this chapter, we focus on databases and Internet-based guidelines and information resources created or written for a professional audience.

NIH Guidelines

Commonly referred to as "clinical" or "professional" guidelines, the National Institutes of Health publish physician guidelines for the most common diseases. Publications are available at the following by relevant Institute[10]:

- Office of the Director (OD); guidelines consolidated across agencies available at **http://www.nih.gov/health/consumer/conkey.htm**

- National Institute of General Medical Sciences (NIGMS); fact sheets available at **http://www.nigms.nih.gov/news/facts/**

- National Library of Medicine (NLM); extensive encyclopedia (A.D.A.M., Inc.) with guidelines: **http://www.nlm.nih.gov/medlineplus/healthtopics.html**

- National Cancer Institute (NCI); guidelines available at **http://www.cancer.gov/cancerinfo/list.aspx?viewid=5f35036e-5497-4d86-8c2c-714a9f7c8d25**

- National Eye Institute (NEI); guidelines available at **http://www.nei.nih.gov/order/index.htm**

- National Heart, Lung, and Blood Institute (NHLBI); guidelines available at **http://www.nhlbi.nih.gov/guidelines/index.htm**

- National Human Genome Research Institute (NHGRI); research available at **http://www.genome.gov/page.cfm?pageID=10000375**

- National Institute on Aging (NIA); guidelines available at **http://www.nia.nih.gov/health/**

---

[10] These publications are typically written by one or more of the various NIH Institutes.

- National Institute on Alcohol Abuse and Alcoholism (NIAAA); guidelines available at **http://www.niaaa.nih.gov/publications/publications.htm**

- National Institute of Allergy and Infectious Diseases (NIAID); guidelines available at **http://www.niaid.nih.gov/publications/**

- National Institute of Arthritis and Musculoskeletal and Skin Diseases (NIAMS); fact sheets and guidelines available at **http://www.niams.nih.gov/hi/index.htm**

- National Institute of Child Health and Human Development (NICHD); guidelines available at **http://www.nichd.nih.gov/publications/pubskey.cfm**

- National Institute on Deafness and Other Communication Disorders (NIDCD); fact sheets and guidelines at **http://www.nidcd.nih.gov/health/**

- National Institute of Dental and Craniofacial Research (NIDCR); guidelines available at **http://www.nidr.nih.gov/health/**

- National Institute of Diabetes and Digestive and Kidney Diseases (NIDDK); guidelines available at **http://www.niddk.nih.gov/health/health.htm**

- National Institute on Drug Abuse (NIDA); guidelines available at **http://www.nida.nih.gov/DrugAbuse.html**

- National Institute of Environmental Health Sciences (NIEHS); environmental health information available at **http://www.niehs.nih.gov/external/facts.htm**

- National Institute of Mental Health (NIMH); guidelines available at **http://www.nimh.nih.gov/practitioners/index.cfm**

- National Institute of Neurological Disorders and Stroke (NINDS); neurological disorder information pages available at **http://www.ninds.nih.gov/health_and_medical/disorder_index.htm**

- National Institute of Nursing Research (NINR); publications on selected illnesses at **http://www.nih.gov/ninr/news-info/publications.html**

- National Institute of Biomedical Imaging and Bioengineering; general information at **http://grants.nih.gov/grants/becon/becon_info.htm**

- Center for Information Technology (CIT); referrals to other agencies based on keyword searches available at **http://kb.nih.gov/www_query_main.asp**

- National Center for Complementary and Alternative Medicine (NCCAM); health information available at **http://nccam.nih.gov/health/**

- National Center for Research Resources (NCRR); various information directories available at **http://www.ncrr.nih.gov/publications.asp**

- Office of Rare Diseases; various fact sheets available at **http://rarediseases.info.nih.gov/html/resources/rep_pubs.html**

- Centers for Disease Control and Prevention; various fact sheets on infectious diseases available at **http://www.cdc.gov/publications.htm**

NIH Databases

In addition to the various Institutes of Health that publish professional guidelines, the NIH has designed a number of databases for professionals.[11] Physician-oriented resources provide a wide variety of information related to the biomedical and health sciences, both past and present. The format of these resources varies. Searchable databases, bibliographic citations, full-text articles (when available), archival collections, and images are all available. The following are referenced by the National Library of Medicine:[12]

- **Bioethics:** Access to published literature on the ethical, legal, and public policy issues surrounding healthcare and biomedical research. This information is provided in conjunction with the Kennedy Institute of Ethics located at Georgetown University, Washington, D.C.: **http://www.nlm.nih.gov/databases/databases_bioethics.html**

- **HIV/AIDS Resources:** Describes various links and databases dedicated to HIV/AIDS research: **http://www.nlm.nih.gov/pubs/factsheets/aidsinfs.html**

- **NLM Online Exhibitions:** Describes "Exhibitions in the History of Medicine": **http://www.nlm.nih.gov/exhibition/exhibition.html**. Additional resources for historical scholarship in medicine: **http://www.nlm.nih.gov/hmd/hmd.html**

- **Biotechnology Information:** Access to public databases. The National Center for Biotechnology Information conducts research in computational biology, develops software tools for analyzing genome data, and disseminates biomedical information for the better understanding of molecular processes affecting human health and disease: **http://www.ncbi.nlm.nih.gov/**

- **Population Information:** The National Library of Medicine provides access to worldwide coverage of population, family planning, and related health issues, including family planning technology and programs, fertility, and population law and policy: **http://www.nlm.nih.gov/databases/databases_population.html**

- **Cancer Information:** Access to cancer-oriented databases: **http://www.nlm.nih.gov/databases/databases_cancer.html**

- **Profiles in Science:** Offering the archival collections of prominent twentieth-century biomedical scientists to the public through modern digital technology: **http://www.profiles.nlm.nih.gov/**

- **Chemical Information:** Provides links to various chemical databases and references: **http://sis.nlm.nih.gov/Chem/ChemMain.html**

- **Clinical Alerts:** Reports the release of findings from the NIH-funded clinical trials where such release could significantly affect morbidity and mortality: **http://www.nlm.nih.gov/databases/alerts/clinical_alerts.html**

- **Space Life Sciences:** Provides links and information to space-based research (including NASA): **http://www.nlm.nih.gov/databases/databases_space.html**

- **MEDLINE:** Bibliographic database covering the fields of medicine, nursing, dentistry, veterinary medicine, the healthcare system, and the pre-clinical sciences: **http://www.nlm.nih.gov/databases/databases_medline.html**

---

[11] Remember, for the general public, the National Library of Medicine recommends the databases referenced in MEDLINE*plus* (http://medlineplus.gov/ or http://www.nlm.nih.gov/medlineplus/databases.html).

[12] See **http://www.nlm.nih.gov/databases/databases.html**.

- **Toxicology and Environmental Health Information (TOXNET):** Databases covering toxicology and environmental health: **http://sis.nlm.nih.gov/Tox/ToxMain.html**

- **Visible Human Interface:** Anatomically detailed, three-dimensional representations of normal male and female human bodies: **http://www.nlm.nih.gov/research/visible/visible_human.html**

The NLM Gateway[13]

The NLM (National Library of Medicine) Gateway is a Web-based system that lets users search simultaneously in multiple retrieval systems at the U.S. National Library of Medicine (NLM). It allows users of NLM services to initiate searches from one Web interface, providing one-stop searching for many of NLM's information resources or databases.[14] To use the NLM Gateway, simply go to the search site at **http://gateway.nlm.nih.gov/gw/Cmd**. Type "Prozac" (or synonyms) into the search box and click "Search." The results will be presented in a tabular form, indicating the number of references in each database category.

Results Summary

Category	Items Found
Journal Articles	4352
Books / Periodicals / Audio Visual	40
Consumer Health	119
Meeting Abstracts	23
Other Collections	8
Total	4542

HSTAT[15]

HSTAT is a free, Web-based resource that provides access to full-text documents used in healthcare decision-making.[16] These documents include clinical practice guidelines, quick-reference guides for clinicians, consumer health brochures, evidence reports and technology assessments from the Agency for Healthcare Research and Quality (AHRQ), as well as AHRQ's Put Prevention Into Practice.[17] Simply search by "Prozac" (or synonyms) at the following Web site: **http://text.nlm.nih.gov**.

---

[13] Adapted from NLM: **http://gateway.nlm.nih.gov/gw/Cmd?Overview.x**.

[14] The NLM Gateway is currently being developed by the Lister Hill National Center for Biomedical Communications (LHNCBC) at the National Library of Medicine (NLM) of the National Institutes of Health (NIH).

[15] Adapted from HSTAT: **http://www.nlm.nih.gov/pubs/factsheets/hstat.html**.

[16] The HSTAT URL is **http://hstat.nlm.nih.gov/**.

[17] Other important documents in HSTAT include: the National Institutes of Health (NIH) Consensus Conference Reports and Technology Assessment Reports; the HIV/AIDS Treatment Information Service (ATIS) resource documents; the Substance Abuse and Mental Health Services Administration's Center for Substance Abuse Treatment (SAMHSA/CSAT) Treatment Improvement Protocols (TIP) and Center for Substance Abuse Prevention (SAMHSA/CSAP) Prevention Enhancement Protocols System (PEPS); the Public Health Service (PHS) Preventive Services Task Force's *Guide to Clinical Preventive Services*; the independent, nonfederal Task Force on Community Services' *Guide to Community Preventive Services*; and the Health Technology Advisory Committee (HTAC) of the Minnesota Health Care Commission (MHCC) health technology evaluations.

Coffee Break: Tutorials for Biologists[18]

Coffee Break is a general healthcare site that takes a scientific view of the news and covers recent breakthroughs in biology that may one day assist physicians in developing treatments. Here you will find a collection of short reports on recent biological discoveries. Each report incorporates interactive tutorials that demonstrate how bioinformatics tools are used as a part of the research process. Currently, all Coffee Breaks are written by NCBI staff.[19] Each report is about 400 words and is usually based on a discovery reported in one or more articles from recently published, peer-reviewed literature.[20] This site has new articles every few weeks, so it can be considered an online magazine of sorts. It is intended for general background information. You can access the Coffee Break Web site at the following hyperlink: **http://www.ncbi.nlm.nih.gov/Coffeebreak/.**

Other Commercial Databases

In addition to resources maintained by official agencies, other databases exist that are commercial ventures addressing medical professionals. Here are some examples that may interest you:

- **CliniWeb International:** Index and table of contents to selected clinical information on the Internet; see **http://www.ohsu.edu/cliniweb/.**

- **Medical World Search:** Searches full text from thousands of selected medical sites on the Internet; see **http://www.mwsearch.com/.**

---

[18] Adapted from **http://www.ncbi.nlm.nih.gov/Coffeebreak/Archive/FAQ.html.**

[19] The figure that accompanies each article is frequently supplied by an expert external to NCBI, in which case the source of the figure is cited. The result is an interactive tutorial that tells a biological story.

[20] After a brief introduction that sets the work described into a broader context, the report focuses on how a molecular understanding can provide explanations of observed biology and lead to therapies for diseases. Each vignette is accompanied by a figure and hypertext links that lead to a series of pages that interactively show how NCBI tools and resources are used in the research process.

APPENDIX B. PATIENT RESOURCES

Overview

Official agencies, as well as federally funded institutions supported by national grants, frequently publish a variety of guidelines written with the patient in mind. These are typically called "Fact Sheets" or "Guidelines." They can take the form of a brochure, information kit, pamphlet, or flyer. Often they are only a few pages in length. Since new guidelines on Prozac can appear at any moment and be published by a number of sources, the best approach to finding guidelines is to systematically scan the Internet-based services that post them.

Patient Guideline Sources

The remainder of this chapter directs you to sources which either publish or can help you find additional guidelines on topics related to Prozac. Due to space limitations, these sources are listed in a concise manner. Do not hesitate to consult the following sources by either using the Internet hyperlink provided, or, in cases where the contact information is provided, contacting the publisher or author directly.

The National Institutes of Health

The NIH gateway to patients is located at **http://health.nih.gov/**. From this site, you can search across various sources and institutes, a number of which are summarized below.

Topic Pages: MEDLINEplus

The National Library of Medicine has created a vast and patient-oriented healthcare information portal called MEDLINEplus. Within this Internet-based system are "health topic pages" which list links to available materials relevant to Prozac. To access this system, log on to **http://www.nlm.nih.gov/medlineplus/healthtopics.html**. From there you can either search using the alphabetical index or browse by broad topic areas. Recently, MEDLINEplus listed the following when searched for "Prozac":

- Other guides

  Child Mental Health
  http://www.nlm.nih.gov/medlineplus/childmentalhealth.html

  Mental Health
  http://www.nlm.nih.gov/medlineplus/mentalhealth.html

  Obsessive-Compulsive Disorder
  http://www.nlm.nih.gov/medlineplus/obsessivecompulsivedisorder.html

  Tourette Syndrome
  http://www.nlm.nih.gov/medlineplus/tourettesyndrome.html

You may also choose to use the search utility provided by MEDLINEplus at the following Web address: **http://www.nlm.nih.gov/medlineplus/**. Simply type a keyword into the search box and click "Search." This utility is similar to the NIH search utility, with the exception that it only includes materials that are linked within the MEDLINEplus system (mostly patient-oriented information). It also has the disadvantage of generating unstructured results. We recommend, therefore, that you use this method only if you have a very targeted search.

The NIH Search Utility

The NIH search utility allows you to search for documents on over 100 selected Web sites that comprise the NIH-WEB-SPACE. Each of these servers is "crawled" and indexed on an ongoing basis. Your search will produce a list of various documents, all of which will relate in some way to Prozac. The drawbacks of this approach are that the information is not organized by theme and that the references are often a mix of information for professionals and patients. Nevertheless, a large number of the listed Web sites provide useful background information. We can only recommend this route, therefore, for relatively rare or specific disorders, or when using highly targeted searches. To use the NIH search utility, visit the following Web page: **http://search.nih.gov/index.html**.

Additional Web Sources

A number of Web sites are available to the public that often link to government sites. These can also point you in the direction of essential information. The following is a representative sample:

- AOL: **http://search.aol.com/cat.adp?id=168&layer=&from=subcats**

- Family Village: **http://www.familyvillage.wisc.edu/specific.htm**

- Google: **http://directory.google.com/Top/Health/Conditions_and_Diseases/**

- Med Help International: **http://www.medhelp.org/HealthTopics/A.html**

- Open Directory Project: **http://dmoz.org/Health/Conditions_and_Diseases/**

- Yahoo.com: **http://dir.yahoo.com/Health/Diseases_and_Conditions/**

- WebMD®Health: **http://my.webmd.com/health_topics**

Finding Associations

There are several Internet directories that provide lists of medical associations with information on or resources relating to Prozac. By consulting all of associations listed in this chapter, you will have nearly exhausted all sources for patient associations concerned with Prozac.

The National Health Information Center (NHIC)

The National Health Information Center (NHIC) offers a free referral service to help people find organizations that provide information about Prozac. For more information, see the NHIC's Web site at **http://www.health.gov/NHIC/** or contact an information specialist by calling 1-800-336-4797.

Directory of Health Organizations

The Directory of Health Organizations, provided by the National Library of Medicine Specialized Information Services, is a comprehensive source of information on associations. The Directory of Health Organizations database can be accessed via the Internet at **http://www.sis.nlm.nih.gov/Dir/DirMain.html**. It is composed of two parts: DIRLINE and Health Hotlines.

The DIRLINE database comprises some 10,000 records of organizations, research centers, and government institutes and associations that primarily focus on health and biomedicine. To access DIRLINE directly, go to the following Web site: **http://dirline.nlm.nih.gov/**. Simply type in "Prozac" (or a synonym), and you will receive information on all relevant organizations listed in the database.

Health Hotlines directs you to toll-free numbers to over 300 organizations. You can access this database directly at **http://www.sis.nlm.nih.gov/hotlines/**. On this page, you are given the option to search by keyword or by browsing the subject list. When you have received your search results, click on the name of the organization for its description and contact information.

The Combined Health Information Database

Another comprehensive source of information on healthcare associations is the Combined Health Information Database. Using the "Detailed Search" option, you will need to limit your search to "Organizations" and "Prozac". Type the following hyperlink into your Web browser: **http://chid.nih.gov/detail/detail.html**. To find associations, use the drop boxes at the bottom of the search page where "You may refine your search by." For publication date, select "All Years." Then, select your preferred language and the format option "Organization Resource Sheet." Type "Prozac" (or synonyms) into the "For these words:" box. You should check back periodically with this database since it is updated every three months.

The National Organization for Rare Disorders, Inc.

The National Organization for Rare Disorders, Inc. has prepared a Web site that provides, at no charge, lists of associations organized by health topic. You can access this database at the following Web site: **http://www.rarediseases.org/search/orgsearch.html**. Type "Prozac" (or a synonym) into the search box, and click "Submit Query."

APPENDIX C. FINDING MEDICAL LIBRARIES

Overview

In this Appendix, we show you how to quickly find a medical library in your area.

Preparation

Your local public library and medical libraries have interlibrary loan programs with the National Library of Medicine (NLM), one of the largest medical collections in the world. According to the NLM, most of the literature in the general and historical collections of the National Library of Medicine is available on interlibrary loan to any library. If you would like to access NLM medical literature, then visit a library in your area that can request the publications for you.[21]

Finding a Local Medical Library

The quickest method to locate medical libraries is to use the Internet-based directory published by the National Network of Libraries of Medicine (NN/LM). This network includes 4626 members and affiliates that provide many services to librarians, health professionals, and the public. To find a library in your area, simply visit **http://nnlm.gov/members/adv.html** or call 1-800-338-7657.

Medical Libraries in the U.S. and Canada

In addition to the NN/LM, the National Library of Medicine (NLM) lists a number of libraries with reference facilities that are open to the public. The following is the NLM's list and includes hyperlinks to each library's Web site. These Web pages can provide information on hours of operation and other restrictions. The list below is a small sample of

---

[21] Adapted from the NLM: **http://www.nlm.nih.gov/psd/cas/interlibrary.html**.

libraries recommended by the National Library of Medicine (sorted alphabetically by name of the U.S. state or Canadian province where the library is located)[22]:

- **Alabama:** Health InfoNet of Jefferson County (Jefferson County Library Cooperative, Lister Hill Library of the Health Sciences), **http://www.uab.edu/infonet/**
- **Alabama:** Richard M. Scrushy Library (American Sports Medicine Institute)
- **Arizona:** Samaritan Regional Medical Center: The Learning Center (Samaritan Health System, Phoenix, Arizona), **http://www.samaritan.edu/library/bannerlibs.htm**
- **California:** Kris Kelly Health Information Center (St. Joseph Health System, Humboldt), **http://www.humboldt1.com/~kkhic/index.html**
- **California:** Community Health Library of Los Gatos, **http://www.healthlib.org/orgresources.html**
- **California:** Consumer Health Program and Services (CHIPS) (County of Los Angeles Public Library, Los Angeles County Harbor-UCLA Medical Center Library) - Carson, CA, **http://www.colapublib.org/services/chips.html**
- **California:** Gateway Health Library (Sutter Gould Medical Foundation)
- **California:** Health Library (Stanford University Medical Center), **http://www-med.stanford.edu/healthlibrary/**
- **California:** Patient Education Resource Center - Health Information and Resources (University of California, San Francisco), **http://sfghdean.ucsf.edu/barnett/PERC/default.asp**
- **California:** Redwood Health Library (Petaluma Health Care District), **http://www.phcd.org/rdwdlib.html**
- **California:** Los Gatos PlaneTree Health Library, **http://planetreesanjose.org/**
- **California:** Sutter Resource Library (Sutter Hospitals Foundation, Sacramento), **http://suttermedicalcenter.org/library/**
- **California:** Health Sciences Libraries (University of California, Davis), **http://www.lib.ucdavis.edu/healthsci/**
- **California:** ValleyCare Health Library & Ryan Comer Cancer Resource Center (ValleyCare Health System, Pleasanton), **http://gaelnet.stmarys-ca.edu/other.libs/gbal/east/vchl.html**
- **California:** Washington Community Health Resource Library (Fremont), **http://www.healthlibrary.org/**
- **Colorado:** William V. Gervasini Memorial Library (Exempla Healthcare), **http://www.saintjosephdenver.org/yourhealth/libraries/**
- **Connecticut:** Hartford Hospital Health Science Libraries (Hartford Hospital), **http://www.harthosp.org/library/**
- **Connecticut:** Healthnet: Connecticut Consumer Health Information Center (University of Connecticut Health Center, Lyman Maynard Stowe Library), **http://library.uchc.edu/departm/hnet/**

---

[22] Abstracted from **http://www.nlm.nih.gov/medlineplus/libraries.html**.

- **Connecticut:** Waterbury Hospital Health Center Library (Waterbury Hospital, Waterbury), **http://www.waterburyhospital.com/library/consumer.shtml**

- **Delaware:** Consumer Health Library (Christiana Care Health System, Eugene du Pont Preventive Medicine & Rehabilitation Institute, Wilmington), **http://www.christianacare.org/health_guide/health_guide_pmri_health_info.cfm**

- **Delaware:** Lewis B. Flinn Library (Delaware Academy of Medicine, Wilmington), **http://www.delamed.org/chls.html**

- **Georgia:** Family Resource Library (Medical College of Georgia, Augusta), **http://cmc.mcg.edu/kids_families/fam_resources/fam_res_lib/frl.htm**

- **Georgia:** Health Resource Center (Medical Center of Central Georgia, Macon), **http://www.mccg.org/hrc/hrchome.asp**

- **Hawaii:** Hawaii Medical Library: Consumer Health Information Service (Hawaii Medical Library, Honolulu), **http://hml.org/CHIS/**

- **Idaho:** DeArmond Consumer Health Library (Kootenai Medical Center, Coeur d'Alene), **http://www.nicon.org/DeArmond/index.htm**

- **Illinois:** Health Learning Center of Northwestern Memorial Hospital (Chicago), **http://www.nmh.org/health_info/hlc.html**

- **Illinois:** Medical Library (OSF Saint Francis Medical Center, Peoria), **http://www.osfsaintfrancis.org/general/library/**

- **Kentucky:** Medical Library - Services for Patients, Families, Students & the Public (Central Baptist Hospital, Lexington), **http://www.centralbap.com/education/community/library.cfm**

- **Kentucky:** University of Kentucky - Health Information Library (Chandler Medical Center, Lexington), **http://www.mc.uky.edu/PatientEd/**

- **Louisiana:** Alton Ochsner Medical Foundation Library (Alton Ochsner Medical Foundation, New Orleans), **http://www.ochsner.org/library/**

- **Louisiana:** Louisiana State University Health Sciences Center Medical Library-Shreveport, **http://lib-sh.lsuhsc.edu/**

- **Maine:** Franklin Memorial Hospital Medical Library (Franklin Memorial Hospital, Farmington), **http://www.fchn.org/fmh/lib.htm**

- **Maine:** Gerrish-True Health Sciences Library (Central Maine Medical Center, Lewiston), **http://www.cmmc.org/library/library.html**

- **Maine:** Hadley Parrot Health Science Library (Eastern Maine Healthcare, Bangor), **http://www.emh.org/hll/hpl/guide.htm**

- **Maine:** Maine Medical Center Library (Maine Medical Center, Portland), **http://www.mmc.org/library/**

- **Maine:** Parkview Hospital (Brunswick), **http://www.parkviewhospital.org/**

- **Maine:** Southern Maine Medical Center Health Sciences Library (Southern Maine Medical Center, Biddeford), **http://www.smmc.org/services/service.php3?choice=10**

- **Maine:** Stephens Memorial Hospital's Health Information Library (Western Maine Health, Norway), **http://www.wmhcc.org/Library/**

- **Manitoba, Canada:** Consumer & Patient Health Information Service (University of Manitoba Libraries), http://www.umanitoba.ca/libraries/units/health/reference/chis.html

- **Manitoba, Canada:** J.W. Crane Memorial Library (Deer Lodge Centre, Winnipeg), http://www.deerlodge.mb.ca/crane_library/about.asp

- **Maryland:** Health Information Center at the Wheaton Regional Library (Montgomery County, Dept. of Public Libraries, Wheaton Regional Library), http://www.mont.lib.md.us/healthinfo/hic.asp

- **Massachusetts:** Baystate Medical Center Library (Baystate Health System), http://www.baystatehealth.com/1024/

- **Massachusetts:** Boston University Medical Center Alumni Medical Library (Boston University Medical Center), http://med-libwww.bu.edu/library/lib.html

- **Massachusetts:** Lowell General Hospital Health Sciences Library (Lowell General Hospital, Lowell), http://www.lowellgeneral.org/library/HomePageLinks/WWW.htm

- **Massachusetts:** Paul E. Woodard Health Sciences Library (New England Baptist Hospital, Boston), http://www.nebh.org/health_lib.asp

- **Massachusetts:** St. Luke's Hospital Health Sciences Library (St. Luke's Hospital, Southcoast Health System, New Bedford), http://www.southcoast.org/library/

- **Massachusetts:** Treadwell Library Consumer Health Reference Center (Massachusetts General Hospital), http://www.mgh.harvard.edu/library/chrcindex.html

- **Massachusetts:** UMass HealthNet (University of Massachusetts Medical School, Worchester), http://healthnet.umassmed.edu/

- **Michigan:** Botsford General Hospital Library - Consumer Health (Botsford General Hospital, Library & Internet Services), http://www.botsfordlibrary.org/consumer.htm

- **Michigan:** Helen DeRoy Medical Library (Providence Hospital and Medical Centers), http://www.providence-hospital.org/library/

- **Michigan:** Marquette General Hospital - Consumer Health Library (Marquette General Hospital, Health Information Center), http://www.mgh.org/center.html

- **Michigan:** Patient Education Resouce Center - University of Michigan Cancer Center (University of Michigan Comprehensive Cancer Center, Ann Arbor), http://www.cancer.med.umich.edu/learn/leares.htm

- **Michigan:** Sladen Library & Center for Health Information Resources - Consumer Health Information (Detroit), http://www.henryford.com/body.cfm?id=39330

- **Montana:** Center for Health Information (St. Patrick Hospital and Health Sciences Center, Missoula)

- **National:** Consumer Health Library Directory (Medical Library Association, Consumer and Patient Health Information Section), http://caphis.mlanet.org/directory/index.html

- **National:** National Network of Libraries of Medicine (National Library of Medicine) - provides library services for health professionals in the United States who do not have access to a medical library, http://nnlm.gov/

- **National:** NN/LM List of Libraries Serving the Public (National Network of Libraries of Medicine), http://nnlm.gov/members/

- **Nevada:** Health Science Library, West Charleston Library (Las Vegas-Clark County Library District, Las Vegas), http://www.lvccld.org/special_collections/medical/index.htm

- **New Hampshire:** Dartmouth Biomedical Libraries (Dartmouth College Library, Hanover), http://www.dartmouth.edu/~biomed/resources.htmld/conshealth.htmld/

- **New Jersey:** Consumer Health Library (Rahway Hospital, Rahway), http://www.rahwayhospital.com/library.htm

- **New Jersey:** Dr. Walter Phillips Health Sciences Library (Englewood Hospital and Medical Center, Englewood), http://www.englewoodhospital.com/links/index.htm

- **New Jersey:** Meland Foundation (Englewood Hospital and Medical Center, Englewood), http://www.geocities.com/ResearchTriangle/9360/

- **New York:** Choices in Health Information (New York Public Library) - NLM Consumer Pilot Project participant, http://www.nypl.org/branch/health/links.html

- **New York:** Health Information Center (Upstate Medical University, State University of New York, Syracuse), http://www.upstate.edu/library/hic/

- **New York:** Health Sciences Library (Long Island Jewish Medical Center, New Hyde Park), http://www.lij.edu/library/library.html

- **New York:** ViaHealth Medical Library (Rochester General Hospital), http://www.nyam.org/library/

- **Ohio:** Consumer Health Library (Akron General Medical Center, Medical & Consumer Health Library), http://www.akrongeneral.org/hwlibrary.htm

- **Oklahoma:** The Health Information Center at Saint Francis Hospital (Saint Francis Health System, Tulsa), http://www.sfh-tulsa.com/services/healthinfo.asp

- **Oregon:** Planetree Health Resource Center (Mid-Columbia Medical Center, The Dalles), http://www.mcmc.net/phrc/

- **Pennsylvania:** Community Health Information Library (Milton S. Hershey Medical Center, Hershey), http://www.hmc.psu.edu/commhealth/

- **Pennsylvania:** Community Health Resource Library (Geisinger Medical Center, Danville), http://www.geisinger.edu/education/commlib.shtml

- **Pennsylvania:** HealthInfo Library (Moses Taylor Hospital, Scranton), http://www.mth.org/healthwellness.html

- **Pennsylvania:** Hopwood Library (University of Pittsburgh, Health Sciences Library System, Pittsburgh), http://www.hsls.pitt.edu/guides/chi/hopwood/index_html

- **Pennsylvania:** Koop Community Health Information Center (College of Physicians of Philadelphia), http://www.collphyphil.org/kooppg1.shtml

- **Pennsylvania:** Learning Resources Center - Medical Library (Susquehanna Health System, Williamsport), http://www.shscares.org/services/lrc/index.asp

- **Pennsylvania:** Medical Library (UPMC Health System, Pittsburgh), http://www.upmc.edu/passavant/library.htm

- **Quebec, Canada:** Medical Library (Montreal General Hospital), http://www.mghlib.mcgill.ca/

- **South Dakota:** Rapid City Regional Hospital Medical Library (Rapid City Regional Hospital), **http://www.rcrh.org/Services/Library/Default.asp**

- **Texas:** Houston HealthWays (Houston Academy of Medicine-Texas Medical Center Library), **http://hhw.library.tmc.edu/**

- **Washington:** Community Health Library (Kittitas Valley Community Hospital), **http://www.kvch.com/**

- **Washington:** Southwest Washington Medical Center Library (Southwest Washington Medical Center, Vancouver), **http://www.swmedicalcenter.com/body.cfm?id=72**

ONLINE GLOSSARIES

The Internet provides access to a number of free-to-use medical dictionaries. The National Library of Medicine has compiled the following list of online dictionaries:

- ADAM Medical Encyclopedia (A.D.A.M., Inc.), comprehensive medical reference: **http://www.nlm.nih.gov/medlineplus/encyclopedia.html**

- MedicineNet.com Medical Dictionary (MedicineNet, Inc.): **http://www.medterms.com/Script/Main/hp.asp**

- Merriam-Webster Medical Dictionary (Inteli-Health, Inc.): **http://www.intelihealth.com/IH/**

- Multilingual Glossary of Technical and Popular Medical Terms in Eight European Languages (European Commission) - Danish, Dutch, English, French, German, Italian, Portuguese, and Spanish: **http://allserv.rug.ac.be/~rvdstich/eugloss/welcome.html**

- On-line Medical Dictionary (CancerWEB): **http://cancerweb.ncl.ac.uk/omd/**

- Rare Diseases Terms (Office of Rare Diseases): **http://ord.aspensys.com/asp/diseases/diseases.asp**

- Technology Glossary (National Library of Medicine) - Health Care Technology: **http://www.nlm.nih.gov/nichsr/ta101/ta10108.htm**

Beyond these, MEDLINEplus contains a very patient-friendly encyclopedia covering every aspect of medicine (licensed from A.D.A.M., Inc.). The ADAM Medical Encyclopedia can be accessed at **http://www.nlm.nih.gov/medlineplus/encyclopedia.html**. ADAM is also available on commercial Web sites such as drkoop.com (**http://www.drkoop.com/**) and Web MD (**http://my.webmd.com/adam/asset/adam_disease_articles/a_to_z/a**).

Online Dictionary Directories

The following are additional online directories compiled by the National Library of Medicine, including a number of specialized medical dictionaries:

- Medical Dictionaries: Medical & Biological (World Health Organization): **http://www.who.int/hlt/virtuallibrary/English/diction.htm#Medical**

- MEL-Michigan Electronic Library List of Online Health and Medical Dictionaries (Michigan Electronic Library): **http://mel.lib.mi.us/health/health-dictionaries.html**

- Patient Education: Glossaries (DMOZ Open Directory Project): **http://dmoz.org/Health/Education/Patient_Education/Glossaries/**

- Web of Online Dictionaries (Bucknell University): **http://www.yourdictionary.com/diction5.html#medicine**

PROZAC DICTIONARY

The definitions below are derived from official public sources, including the National Institutes of Health [NIH] and the European Union [EU].

5,7-Dihydroxytryptamine: Tryptamine substituted with two hydroxyl groups in positions 5 and 7. It is a neurotoxic serotonin analog that destroys serotonergic neurons preferentially and is used in neuropharmacology as a tool. [NIH]

Abdominal: Having to do with the abdomen, which is the part of the body between the chest and the hips that contains the pancreas, stomach, intestines, liver, gallbladder, and other organs. [NIH]

Abortion: 1. The premature expulsion from the uterus of the products of conception - of the embryo, or of a nonviable fetus. The four classic symptoms, usually present in each type of abortion, are uterine contractions, uterine haemorrhage, softening and dilatation of the cervix, and presentation or expulsion of all or part of the products of conception. 2. Premature stoppage of a natural or a pathological process. [EU]

Acetylcholine: A neurotransmitter. Acetylcholine in vertebrates is the major transmitter at neuromuscular junctions, autonomic ganglia, parasympathetic effector junctions, a subset of sympathetic effector junctions, and at many sites in the central nervous system. It is generally not used as an administered drug because it is broken down very rapidly by cholinesterases, but it is useful in some ophthalmological applications. [NIH]

Adaptation: 1. The adjustment of an organism to its environment, or the process by which it enhances such fitness. 2. The normal ability of the eye to adjust itself to variations in the intensity of light; the adjustment to such variations. 3. The decline in the frequency of firing of a neuron, particularly of a receptor, under conditions of constant stimulation. 4. In dentistry, (a) the proper fitting of a denture, (b) the degree of proximity and interlocking of restorative material to a tooth preparation, (c) the exact adjustment of bands to teeth. 5. In microbiology, the adjustment of bacterial physiology to a new environment. [EU]

Adjustment: The dynamic process wherein the thoughts, feelings, behavior, and biophysiological mechanisms of the individual continually change to adjust to the environment. [NIH]

Adrenal Cortex: The outer layer of the adrenal gland. It secretes mineralocorticoids, androgens, and glucocorticoids. [NIH]

Adrenal Medulla: The inner part of the adrenal gland; it synthesizes, stores and releases catecholamines. [NIH]

Adrenergic: Activated by, characteristic of, or secreting epinephrine or substances with similar activity; the term is applied to those nerve fibres that liberate norepinephrine at a synapse when a nerve impulse passes, i.e., the sympathetic fibres. [EU]

Adrenergic Uptake Inhibitors: Drugs that block the transport of adrenergic transmitters into axon terminals or into storage vesicles within terminals. The tricyclic antidepressants (antidepressive agents, tricyclic) and amphetamines are among the therapeutically important drugs that may act via inhibition of adrenergic transport. Many of these drugs also block transport of serotonin. [NIH]

Adverse Effect: An unwanted side effect of treatment. [NIH]

Affinity: 1. Inherent likeness or relationship. 2. A special attraction for a specific element, organ, or structure. 3. Chemical affinity; the force that binds atoms in molecules; the tendency of substances to combine by chemical reaction. 4. The strength of noncovalent chemical binding between two substances as measured by the dissociation constant of the complex. 5. In immunology, a thermodynamic expression of the strength of interaction between a single antigen-binding site and a single antigenic determinant (and thus of the stereochemical compatibility between them), most accurately applied to interactions among simple, uniform antigenic determinants such as haptens. Expressed as the association constant (K litres mole -1), which, owing to the heterogeneity of affinities in a population of antibody molecules of a given specificity, actually represents an average value (mean intrinsic association constant). 6. The reciprocal of the dissociation constant. [EU]

Agenesis: Lack of complete or normal development; congenital absence of an organ or part. [NIH]

Agonist: In anatomy, a prime mover. In pharmacology, a drug that has affinity for and stimulates physiologic activity at cell receptors normally stimulated by naturally occurring substances. [EU]

Agoraphobia: Obsessive, persistent, intense fear of open places. [NIH]

Algorithms: A procedure consisting of a sequence of algebraic formulas and/or logical steps to calculate or determine a given task. [NIH]

Alkaloid: A member of a large group of chemicals that are made by plants and have nitrogen in them. Some alkaloids have been shown to work against cancer. [NIH]

Alkylation: The covalent bonding of an alkyl group to an organic compound. It can occur by a simple addition reaction or by substitution of another functional group. [NIH]

Allergen: An antigenic substance capable of producing immediate-type hypersensitivity (allergy). [EU]

Allylamine: Possesses an unusual and selective cytotoxicity for vascular smooth muscle cells in dogs and rats. Useful for experiments dealing with arterial injury, myocardial fibrosis or cardiac decompensation. [NIH]

Alternative medicine: Practices not generally recognized by the medical community as standard or conventional medical approaches and used instead of standard treatments. Alternative medicine includes the taking of dietary supplements, megadose vitamins, and herbal preparations; the drinking of special teas; and practices such as massage therapy, magnet therapy, spiritual healing, and meditation. [NIH]

Alveolar Process: The thickest and spongiest part of the maxilla and mandible hollowed out into deep cavities for the teeth. [NIH]

Amine: An organic compound containing nitrogen; any member of a group of chemical compounds formed from ammonia by replacement of one or more of the hydrogen atoms by organic (hydrocarbon) radicals. The amines are distinguished as primary, secondary, and tertiary, according to whether one, two, or three hydrogen atoms are replaced. The amines include allylamine, amylamine, ethylamine, methylamine, phenylamine, propylamine, and many other compounds. [EU]

Amino acid: Any organic compound containing an amino (-NH2 and a carboxyl (- COOH) group. The 20 a-amino acids listed in the accompanying table are the amino acids from which proteins are synthesized by formation of peptide bonds during ribosomal translation of messenger RNA; all except glycine, which is not optically active, have the L configuration. Other amino acids occurring in proteins, such as hydroxyproline in collagen, are formed by posttranslational enzymatic modification of amino acids residues in polypeptide chains. There are also several important amino acids, such as the neurotransmitter y-aminobutyric acid, that have no relation to proteins. Abbreviated AA. [EU]

Ammonia: A colorless alkaline gas. It is formed in the body during decomposition of organic materials during a large number of metabolically important reactions. [NIH]

Amphetamine: A powerful central nervous system stimulant and sympathomimetic. Amphetamine has multiple mechanisms of action including blocking uptake of adrenergics and dopamine, stimulation of release of monamines, and inhibiting monoamine oxidase. Amphetamine is also a drug of abuse and a psychotomimetic. The l- and the d,l-forms are included here. The l-form has less central nervous system activity but stronger cardiovascular effects. The d-form is dextroamphetamine. [NIH]

Amygdala: Almond-shaped group of basal nuclei anterior to the inferior horn of the lateral ventricle of the brain, within the temporal lobe. The amygdala is part of the limbic system. [NIH]

Anal: Having to do with the anus, which is the posterior opening of the large bowel. [NIH]

Analgesics: Compounds capable of relieving pain without the loss of consciousness or without producing anesthesia. [NIH]

Analog: In chemistry, a substance that is similar, but not identical, to another. [NIH]

Anatomical: Pertaining to anatomy, or to the structure of the organism. [EU]

Anesthesia: A state characterized by loss of feeling or sensation. This depression of nerve function is usually the result of pharmacologic action and is induced to allow performance of surgery or other painful procedures. [NIH]

Angioid Streaks: Small breaks in the elastin-filled tissue of the retina. [NIH]

Animal model: An animal with a disease either the same as or like a disease in humans. Animal models are used to study the development and progression of diseases and to test new treatments before they are given to humans. Animals with transplanted human cancers or other tissues are called xenograft models. [NIH]

Anions: Negatively charged atoms, radicals or groups of atoms which travel to the anode or positive pole during electrolysis. [NIH]

Anorexia: Lack or loss of appetite for food. Appetite is psychologic, dependent on memory and associations. Anorexia can be brought about by unattractive food, surroundings, or company. [NIH]

Antibody: A type of protein made by certain white blood cells in response to a foreign substance (antigen). Each antibody can bind to only a specific antigen. The purpose of this binding is to help destroy the antigen. Antibodies can work in several ways, depending on the nature of the antigen. Some antibodies destroy antigens directly. Others make it easier for white blood cells to destroy the antigen. [NIH]

Anticonvulsant: An agent that prevents or relieves convulsions. [EU]

Antidepressant: A drug used to treat depression. [NIH]

Antigen: Any substance which is capable, under appropriate conditions, of inducing a specific immune response and of reacting with the products of that response, that is, with specific antibody or specifically sensitized T-lymphocytes, or both. Antigens may be soluble substances, such as toxins and foreign proteins, or particulate, such as bacteria and tissue cells; however, only the portion of the protein or polysaccharide molecule known as the antigenic determinant (q.v.) combines with antibody or a specific receptor on a lymphocyte. Abbreviated Ag. [EU]

Anxiety: Persistent feeling of dread, apprehension, and impending disaster. [NIH]

Anxiety Disorders: Disorders in which anxiety (persistent feelings of apprehension, tension, or uneasiness) is the predominant disturbance. [NIH]

Anxiolytic: An anxiolytic or antianxiety agent. [EU]

Aqueous: Having to do with water. [NIH]

Arachidonic Acid: An unsaturated, essential fatty acid. It is found in animal and human fat as well as in the liver, brain, and glandular organs, and is a constituent of animal phosphatides. It is formed by the synthesis from dietary linoleic acid and is a precursor in the biosynthesis of prostaglandins, thromboxanes, and leukotrienes. [NIH]

Aromatic: Having a spicy odour. [EU]

Arterial: Pertaining to an artery or to the arteries. [EU]

Arteries: The vessels carrying blood away from the heart. [NIH]

Astrocytes: The largest and most numerous neuroglial cells in the brain and spinal cord. Astrocytes (from "star" cells) are irregularly shaped with many long processes, including those with "end feet" which form the glial (limiting) membrane and directly and indirectly contribute to the blood brain barrier. They regulate the extracellular ionic and chemical environment, and "reactive astrocytes" (along with microglia) respond to injury. Astrocytes have high- affinity transmitter uptake systems, voltage-dependent and transmitter-gated ion channels, and can release transmitter, but their role in signaling (as in many other functions) is not well understood. [NIH]

Atrial: Pertaining to an atrium. [EU]

Atrioventricular: Pertaining to an atrium of the heart and to a ventricle. [EU]

Atrium: A chamber; used in anatomical nomenclature to designate a chamber affording entrance to another structure or organ. Usually used alone to designate an atrium of the heart. [EU]

Atypical: Irregular; not conformable to the type; in microbiology, applied specifically to strains of unusual type. [EU]

Autonomic: Self-controlling; functionally independent. [EU]

Bacteria: Unicellular prokaryotic microorganisms which generally possess rigid cell walls, multiply by cell division, and exhibit three principal forms: round or coccal, rodlike or bacillary, and spiral or spirochetal. [NIH]

Bacterial Physiology: Physiological processes and activities of bacteria. [NIH]

Bacteriophage: A virus whose host is a bacterial cell; A virus that exclusively infects bacteria. It generally has a protein coat surrounding the genome (DNA or RNA). One of the coliphages most extensively studied is the lambda phage, which is also one of the most important. [NIH]

Base: In chemistry, the nonacid part of a salt; a substance that combines with acids to form salts; a substance that dissociates to give hydroxide ions in aqueous solutions; a substance whose molecule or ion can combine with a proton (hydrogen ion); a substance capable of donating a pair of electrons (to an acid) for the formation of a coordinate covalent bond. [EU]

Behavior Therapy: The application of modern theories of learning and conditioning in the treatment of behavior disorders. [NIH]

Benzene: Toxic, volatile, flammable liquid hydrocarbon biproduct of coal distillation. It is used as an industrial solvent in paints, varnishes, lacquer thinners, gasoline, etc. Benzene causes central nervous system damage acutely and bone marrow damage chronically and is carcinogenic. It was formerly used as parasiticide. [NIH]

Benzodiazepines: A two-ring heterocyclic compound consisting of a benzene ring fused to a diazepine ring. Permitted is any degree of hydrogenation, any substituents and any H-isomer. [NIH]

Binding Sites: The reactive parts of a macromolecule that directly participate in its specific combination with another molecule. [NIH]

Biochemical: Relating to biochemistry; characterized by, produced by, or involving chemical reactions in living organisms. [EU]

Biotechnology: Body of knowledge related to the use of organisms, cells or cell-derived constituents for the purpose of developing products which are technically, scientifically and clinically useful. Alteration of biologic function at the molecular level (i.e., genetic engineering) is a central focus; laboratory methods used include transfection and cloning technologies, sequence and structure analysis algorithms, computer databases, and gene and protein structure function analysis and prediction. [NIH]

Bladder: The organ that stores urine. [NIH]

Blood Platelets: Non-nucleated disk-shaped cells formed in the megakaryocyte and found in the blood of all mammals. They are mainly involved in blood coagulation. [NIH]

Blood pressure: The pressure of blood against the walls of a blood vessel or heart chamber. Unless there is reference to another location, such as the pulmonary artery or one of the heart chambers, it refers to the pressure in the systemic arteries, as measured, for example, in the forearm. [NIH]

Blood vessel: A tube in the body through which blood circulates. Blood vessels include a network of arteries, arterioles, capillaries, venules, and veins. [NIH]

Body Image: Individuals' personal concept of their bodies as objects in and bound by space, independently and apart from all other objects. [NIH]

Bone Resorption: Bone loss due to osteoclastic activity. [NIH]

Borohydrides: A class of inorganic or organic compounds that contain the borohydride (BH4-) anion. [NIH]

Boron: A trace element with the atomic symbol B, atomic number 5, and atomic weight 10.81. Boron-10, an isotope of boron, is used as a neutron absorber in boron neutron capture therapy. [NIH]

Boron Neutron Capture Therapy: A technique for the treatment of neoplasms, especially gliomas and melanomas in which boron-10, an isotope, is introduced into the target cells followed by irradiation with thermal neutrons. [NIH]

Bowel: The long tube-shaped organ in the abdomen that completes the process of digestion. There is both a small and a large bowel. Also called the intestine. [NIH]

Bowel Movement: Body wastes passed through the rectum and anus. [NIH]

Branch: Most commonly used for branches of nerves, but applied also to other structures. [NIH]

Breakdown: A physical, metal, or nervous collapse. [NIH]

Bulimia: Episodic binge eating. The episodes may be associated with the fear of not being able to stop eating, depressed mood, or self-deprecating thoughts (binge-eating disorder) and may frequently be terminated by self-induced vomiting (bulimia nervosa). [NIH]

Bupropion: A unicyclic, aminoketone antidepressant. The mechanism of its therapeutic actions is not well understood, but it does appear to block dopamine uptake. The hydrochloride is available as an aid to smoking cessation treatment. [NIH]

Calcium: A basic element found in nearly all organized tissues. It is a member of the alkaline earth family of metals with the atomic symbol Ca, atomic number 20, and atomic weight 40. Calcium is the most abundant mineral in the body and combines with phosphorus to form calcium phosphate in the bones and teeth. It is essential for the normal functioning of nerves and muscles and plays a role in blood coagulation (as factor IV) and in many enzymatic processes. [NIH]

Capsules: Hard or soft soluble containers used for the oral administration of medicine. [NIH]

Carbohydrates: The largest class of organic compounds, including starches, glycogens, cellulose, gums, and simple sugars. Carbohydrates are composed of carbon, hydrogen, and oxygen in a ratio of Cn(H2O)n. [NIH]

Carbon Dioxide: A colorless, odorless gas that can be formed by the body and is necessary for the respiration cycle of plants and animals. [NIH]

Cardiac: Having to do with the heart. [NIH]

Cardiovascular: Having to do with the heart and blood vessels. [NIH]

Cardiovascular System: The heart and the blood vessels by which blood is pumped and circulated through the body. [NIH]

Case report: A detailed report of the diagnosis, treatment, and follow-up of an individual patient. Case reports also contain some demographic information about the patient (for example, age, gender, ethnic origin). [NIH]

Catecholamine: A group of chemical substances manufactured by the adrenal medulla and secreted during physiological stress. [NIH]

Cations: Postively charged atoms, radicals or groups of atoms which travel to the cathode or negative pole during electrolysis. [NIH]

Caudal: Denoting a position more toward the cauda, or tail, than some specified point of reference; same as inferior, in human anatomy. [EU]

Cell: The individual unit that makes up all of the tissues of the body. All living things are made up of one or more cells. [NIH]

Cell Differentiation: Progressive restriction of the developmental potential and increasing specialization of function which takes place during the development of the embryo and leads to the formation of specialized cells, tissues, and organs. [NIH]

Cell proliferation: An increase in the number of cells as a result of cell growth and cell division. [NIH]

Cellulose: A polysaccharide with glucose units linked as in cellobiose. It is the chief constituent of plant fibers, cotton being the purest natural form of the substance. As a raw material, it forms the basis for many derivatives used in chromatography, ion exchange materials, explosives manufacturing, and pharmaceutical preparations. [NIH]

Central Nervous System: The main information-processing organs of the nervous system, consisting of the brain, spinal cord, and meninges. [NIH]

Cerebral: Of or pertaining of the cerebrum or the brain. [EU]

Cerebrum: The largest part of the brain. It is divided into two hemispheres, or halves, called the cerebral hemispheres. The cerebrum controls muscle functions of the body and also controls speech, emotions, reading, writing, and learning. [NIH]

Chin: The anatomical frontal portion of the mandible, also known as the mentum, that contains the line of fusion of the two separate halves of the mandible (symphysis menti). This line of fusion divides inferiorly to enclose a triangular area called the mental protuberance. On each side, inferior to the second premolar tooth, is the mental foramen for the passage of blood vessels and a nerve. [NIH]

Cholesterol: The principal sterol of all higher animals, distributed in body tissues, especially the brain and spinal cord, and in animal fats and oils. [NIH]

Chronic: A disease or condition that persists or progresses over a long period of time. [NIH]

Clinical trial: A research study that tests how well new medical treatments or other interventions work in people. Each study is designed to test new methods of screening, prevention, diagnosis, or treatment of a disease. [NIH]

Clonic: Pertaining to or of the nature of clonus. [EU]

Cloning: The production of a number of genetically identical individuals; in genetic engineering, a process for the efficient replication of a geat number of identical DNA molecules. [NIH]

Coca: Any of several South American shrubs of the Erythroxylon genus (and family) that yield cocaine; the leaves are chewed with alum for CNS stimulation. [NIH]

Cocaine: An alkaloid ester extracted from the leaves of plants including coca. It is a local anesthetic and vasoconstrictor and is clinically used for that purpose, particularly in the eye, ear, nose, and throat. It also has powerful central nervous system effects similar to the amphetamines and is a drug of abuse. Cocaine, like amphetamines, acts by multiple mechanisms on brain catecholaminergic neurons; the mechanism of its reinforcing effects is thought to involve inhibition of dopamine uptake. [NIH]

Cofactor: A substance, microorganism or environmental factor that activates or enhances the action of another entity such as a disease-causing agent. [NIH]

Cognition: Intellectual or mental process whereby an organism becomes aware of or obtains knowledge. [NIH]

Collagen: A polypeptide substance comprising about one third of the total protein in mammalian organisms. It is the main constituent of skin, connective tissue, and the organic substance of bones and teeth. Different forms of collagen are produced in the body but all consist of three alpha-polypeptide chains arranged in a triple helix. Collagen is differentiated from other fibrous proteins, such as elastin, by the content of proline, hydroxyproline, and hydroxylysine; by the absence of tryptophan; and particularly by the high content of polar groups which are responsible for its swelling properties. [NIH]

Complement: A term originally used to refer to the heat-labile factor in serum that causes immune cytolysis, the lysis of antibody-coated cells, and now referring to the entire functionally related system comprising at least 20 distinct serum proteins that is the effector not only of immune cytolysis but also of other biologic functions. Complement activation occurs by two different sequences, the classic and alternative pathways. The proteins of the classic pathway are termed 'components of complement' and are designated by the symbols C1 through C9. C1 is a calcium-dependent complex of three distinct proteins C1q, C1r and C1s. The proteins of the alternative pathway (collectively referred to as the properdin system) and complement regulatory proteins are known by semisystematic or trivial names. Fragments resulting from proteolytic cleavage of complement proteins are designated with lower-case letter suffixes, e.g., C3a. Inactivated fragments may be designated with the suffix 'i', e.g. C3bi. Activated components or complexes with biological activity are designated by a bar over the symbol e.g. C1 or C4b,2a. The classic pathway is activated by the binding of C1 to classic pathway activators, primarily antigen-antibody complexes containing IgM, IgG1, IgG3; C1q binds to a single IgM molecule or two adjacent IgG molecules. The alternative pathway can be activated by IgA immune complexes and also by nonimmunologic materials including bacterial endotoxins, microbial polysaccharides, and cell walls. Activation of the classic pathway triggers an enzymatic cascade involving C1, C4, C2 and C3; activation of the alternative pathway triggers a cascade involving C3 and factors B, D and P. Both result in the cleavage of C5 and the formation of the membrane attack complex. Complement activation also results in the formation of many biologically active complement fragments that act as anaphylatoxins, opsonins, or chemotactic factors. [EU]

Complementary and alternative medicine: CAM. Forms of treatment that are used in addition to (complementary) or instead of (alternative) standard treatments. These practices are not considered standard medical approaches. CAM includes dietary supplements, megadose vitamins, herbal preparations, special teas, massage therapy, magnet therapy, spiritual healing, and meditation. [NIH]

Complementary medicine: Practices not generally recognized by the medical community as standard or conventional medical approaches and used to enhance or complement the standard treatments. Complementary medicine includes the taking of dietary supplements, megadose vitamins, and herbal preparations; the drinking of special teas; and practices such as massage therapy, magnet therapy, spiritual healing, and meditation. [NIH]

Compulsions: In psychology, an irresistible urge, sometimes amounting to obsession to perform a particular act which usually is carried out against the performer's will or better judgment. [NIH]

Compulsive Behavior: The behavior of performing an act persistently and repetitively without it leading to reward or pleasure. The act is usually a small, circumscribed behavior, almost ritualistic, yet not pathologically disturbing. Examples of compulsive behavior include twirling of hair, checking something constantly, not wanting pennies in change, straightening tilted pictures, etc. [NIH]

Computational Biology: A field of biology concerned with the development of techniques for the collection and manipulation of biological data, and the use of such data to make biological discoveries or predictions. This field encompasses all computational methods and theories applicable to molecular biology and areas of computer-based techniques for solving biological problems including manipulation of models and datasets. [NIH]

Conception: The onset of pregnancy, marked by implantation of the blastocyst; the formation of a viable zygote. [EU]

Concomitant: Accompanying; accessory; joined with another. [EU]

Connective Tissue: Tissue that supports and binds other tissues. It consists of connective tissue cells embedded in a large amount of extracellular matrix. [NIH]

Connective Tissue: Tissue that supports and binds other tissues. It consists of connective tissue cells embedded in a large amount of extracellular matrix. [NIH]

Connective Tissue Cells: A group of cells that includes fibroblasts, cartilage cells, adipocytes, smooth muscle cells, and bone cells. [NIH]

Consciousness: Sense of awareness of self and of the environment. [NIH]

Constipation: Infrequent or difficult evacuation of feces. [NIH]

Consumption: Pulmonary tuberculosis. [NIH]

Contraindications: Any factor or sign that it is unwise to pursue a certain kind of action or treatment, e. g. giving a general anesthetic to a person with pneumonia. [NIH]

Control group: In a clinical trial, the group that does not receive the new treatment being studied. This group is compared to the group that receives the new treatment, to see if the new treatment works. [NIH]

Controlled study: An experiment or clinical trial that includes a comparison (control) group. [NIH]

Convulsions: A general term referring to sudden and often violent motor activity of cerebral or brainstem origin. Convulsions may also occur in the absence of an electrical cerebral discharge (e.g., in response to hypotension). [NIH]

Cor: The muscular organ that maintains the circulation of the blood. c. adiposum a heart that has undergone fatty degeneration or that has an accumulation of fat around it; called also fat or fatty, heart. c. arteriosum the left side of the heart, so called because it contains oxygenated (arterial) blood. c. biloculare a congenital anomaly characterized by failure of formation of the atrial and ventricular septums, the heart having only two chambers, a single atrium and a single ventricle, and a common atrioventricular valve. c. bovinum (L. 'ox heart') a greatly enlarged heart due to a hypertrophied left ventricle; called also c. taurinum and bucardia. c. dextrum (L. 'right heart') the right atrium and ventricle. c. hirsutum, c. villosum. c. mobile (obs.) an abnormally movable heart. c. pendulum a heart so movable that it seems to be hanging by the great blood vessels. c. pseudotriloculare biatriatum a congenital cardiac anomaly in which the heart functions as a three-chambered heart because of tricuspid atresia, the right ventricle being extremely small or rudimentary and the right atrium greatly dilated. Blood passes from the right to the left atrium and thence disease due to pulmonary hypertension secondary to disease of the lung, or its blood vessels, with hypertrophy of the right ventricle. [EU]

Coronary: Encircling in the manner of a crown; a term applied to vessels; nerves, ligaments, etc. The term usually denotes the arteries that supply the heart muscle and, by extension, a pathologic involvement of them. [EU]

Coronary Thrombosis: Presence of a thrombus in a coronary artery, often causing a myocardial infarction. [NIH]

Corpus: The body of the uterus. [NIH]

Corpus Callosum: Broad plate of dense myelinated fibers that reciprocally interconnect regions of the cortex in all lobes with corresponding regions of the opposite hemisphere. The corpus callosum is located deep in the longitudinal fissure. [NIH]

Corpus Luteum: The yellow glandular mass formed in the ovary by an ovarian follicle that has ruptured and discharged its ovum. [NIH]

Cortex: The outer layer of an organ or other body structure, as distinguished from the internal substance. [EU]

Cortical: Pertaining to or of the nature of a cortex or bark. [EU]

Cortisol: A steroid hormone secreted by the adrenal cortex as part of the body's response to stress. [NIH]

Cytotoxic: Cell-killing. [NIH]

Deamination: The removal of an amino group (NH2) from a chemical compound. [NIH]

Dehydroepiandrosterone: DHEA. A substance that is being studied as a cancer prevention drug. It belongs to the family of drugs called steroids. [NIH]

Deletion: A genetic rearrangement through loss of segments of DNA (chromosomes), bringing sequences, which are normally separated, into close proximity. [NIH]

Dendrites: Extensions of the nerve cell body. They are short and branched and receive stimuli from other neurons. [NIH]

Depersonalization: Alteration in the perception of the self so that the usual sense of one's own reality is lost, manifested in a sense of unreality or self-estrangement, in changes of body image, or in a feeling that one does not control his own actions and speech; seen in depersonalization disorder, schizophrenic disorders, and schizotypal personality disorder. Some do not draw a distinction between depersonalization and derealization, using depersonalization to include both. [EU]

Depolarization: The process or act of neutralizing polarity. In neurophysiology, the reversal of the resting potential in excitable cell membranes when stimulated, i.e., the tendency of the cell membrane potential to become positive with respect to the potential outside the cell. [EU]

Deprenyl: Substance that blocks the breakdown of dopamine, thus preserving its availability in the striatum. [NIH]

Depressive Disorder: An affective disorder manifested by either a dysphoric mood or loss of interest or pleasure in usual activities. The mood disturbance is prominent and relatively persistent. [NIH]

Derealization: Is characterized by the loss of the sense of reality concerning one's surroundings. [NIH]

Desensitization: The prevention or reduction of immediate hypersensitivity reactions by administration of graded doses of allergen; called also hyposensitization and immunotherapy. [EU]

Deuterium: Deuterium. The stable isotope of hydrogen. It has one neutron and one proton in the nucleus. [NIH]

Dextroamphetamine: The d-form of amphetamine. It is a central nervous system stimulant and a sympathomimetic. It has also been used in the treatment of narcolepsy and of attention deficit disorders and hyperactivity in children. Dextroamphetamine has multiple mechanisms of action including blocking uptake of adrenergics and dopamine, stimulating release of monamines, and inhibiting monoamine oxidase. It is also a drug of abuse and a psychotomimetic. [NIH]

Diabetes Mellitus: A heterogeneous group of disorders that share glucose intolerance in common. [NIH]

Diagnostic procedure: A method used to identify a disease. [NIH]

Diencephalon: The paired caudal parts of the prosencephalon from which the thalamus, hypothalamus, epithalamus, and subthalamus are derived. [NIH]

Digestive system: The organs that take in food and turn it into products that the body can use to stay healthy. Waste products the body cannot use leave the body through bowel movements. The digestive system includes the salivary glands, mouth, esophagus, stomach, liver, pancreas, gallbladder, small and large intestines, and rectum. [NIH]

Dihydroprogesterone: 20 alpha-Hydroxypregn-4-en-3-one. A naturally occurring progesterone derivative with progestational activity. [NIH]

Direct: 1. Straight; in a straight line. 2. Performed immediately and without the intervention of subsidiary means. [EU]

Discrete: Made up of separate parts or characterized by lesions which do not become blended; not running together; separate. [NIH]

Discriminant Analysis: A statistical analytic technique used with discrete dependent variables, concerned with separating sets of observed values and allocating new values. It is sometimes used instead of regression analysis. [NIH]

Dissociation: 1. The act of separating or state of being separated. 2. The separation of a molecule into two or more fragments (atoms, molecules, ions, or free radicals) produced by the absorption of light or thermal energy or by solvation. 3. In psychology, a defense mechanism in which a group of mental processes are segregated from the rest of a person's mental activity in order to avoid emotional distress, as in the dissociative disorders (q.v.), or in which an idea or object is segregated from its emotional significance; in the first sense it is roughly equivalent to splitting, in the second, to isolation. 4. A defect of mental integration in which one or more groups of mental processes become separated off from normal consciousness and, thus separated, function as a unitary whole. [EU]

Dizziness: An imprecise term which may refer to a sense of spatial disorientation, motion of the environment, or lightheadedness. [NIH]

Domestic Violence: Deliberate, often repetitive, physical abuse by one family member against another: marital partners, parents, children, siblings, or any other member of a household. [NIH]

Dominance: In genetics, the full phenotypic expression of a gene in both heterozygotes and homozygotes. [EU]

Dopamine: An endogenous catecholamine and prominent neurotransmitter in several systems of the brain. In the synthesis of catecholamines from tyrosine, it is the immediate precursor to norepinephrine and epinephrine. Dopamine is a major transmitter in the extrapyramidal system of the brain, and important in regulating movement. A family of dopaminergic receptor subtypes mediate its action. Dopamine is used pharmacologically for its direct (beta adrenergic agonist) and indirect (adrenergic releasing) sympathomimetic effects including its actions as an inotropic agent and as a renal vasodilator. [NIH]

Dorsal: 1. Pertaining to the back or to any dorsum. 2. Denoting a position more toward the back surface than some other object of reference; same as posterior in human anatomy; superior in the anatomy of quadrupeds. [EU]

Dose-dependent: Refers to the effects of treatment with a drug. If the effects change when the dose of the drug is changed, the effects are said to be dose dependent. [NIH]

Double-blind: Pertaining to a clinical trial or other experiment in which neither the subject nor the person administering treatment knows which treatment any particular subject is receiving. [EU]

Drive: A state of internal activity of an organism that is a necessary condition before a given stimulus will elicit a class of responses; e.g., a certain level of hunger (drive) must be present before food will elicit an eating response. [NIH]

Drug Monitoring: The process of observing, recording, or detecting the effects of a chemical substance administered to an individual therapeutically or diagnostically. [NIH]

Drug Resistance: Diminished or failed response of an organism, disease or tissue to the intended effectiveness of a chemical or drug. It should be differentiated from drug tolerance which is the progressive diminution of the susceptibility of a human or animal to the effects of a drug, as a result of continued administration. [NIH]

Drug Tolerance: Progressive diminution of the susceptibility of a human or animal to the effects of a drug, resulting from its continued administration. It should be differentiated from drug resistance wherein an organism, disease, or tissue fails to respond to the intended effectiveness of a chemical or drug. It should also be differentiated from maximum tolerated dose and no-observed-adverse-effect level. [NIH]

Dysphoric: A feeling of unpleasantness and discomfort. [NIH]

Dyspnea: Difficult or labored breathing. [NIH]

Effector: It is often an enzyme that converts an inactive precursor molecule into an active second messenger. [NIH]

Efficacy: The extent to which a specific intervention, procedure, regimen, or service produces a beneficial result under ideal conditions. Ideally, the determination of efficacy is based on the results of a randomized control trial. [NIH]

Elastic: Susceptible of resisting and recovering from stretching, compression or distortion applied by a force. [EU]

Electrocardiogram: Measurement of electrical activity during heartbeats. [NIH]

Electrolyte: A substance that dissociates into ions when fused or in solution, and thus becomes capable of conducting electricity; an ionic solute. [EU]

Embryo: The prenatal stage of mammalian development characterized by rapid morphological changes and the differentiation of basic structures. [NIH]

Embryo Transfer: Removal of a mammalian embryo from one environment and replacement in the same or a new environment. The embryo is usually in the pre-nidation phase, i.e., a blastocyst. The process includes embryo or blastocyst transplantation or transfer after in vitro fertilization and transfer of the inner cell mass of the blastocyst. It is not used for transfer of differentiated embryonic tissue, e.g., germ layer cells. [NIH]

Empirical: A treatment based on an assumed diagnosis, prior to receiving confirmatory laboratory test results. [NIH]

Endocrine System: The system of glands that release their secretions (hormones) directly into the circulatory system. In addition to the endocrine glands, included are the chromaffin system and the neurosecretory systems. [NIH]

Endogenous: Produced inside an organism or cell. The opposite is external (exogenous) production. [NIH]

Endorphins: One of the three major groups of endogenous opioid peptides. They are large peptides derived from the pro-opiomelanocortin precursor. The known members of this group are alpha-, beta-, and gamma-endorphin. The term endorphin is also sometimes used to refer to all opioid peptides, but the narrower sense is used here; opioid peptides is used for the broader group. [NIH]

Enhancers: Transcriptional element in the virus genome. [NIH]

Enkephalins: One of the three major families of endogenous opioid peptides. The enkephalins are pentapeptides that are widespread in the central and peripheral nervous systems and in the adrenal medulla. [NIH]

Environmental Health: The science of controlling or modifying those conditions, influences, or forces surrounding man which relate to promoting, establishing, and maintaining health. [NIH]

Enzymatic: Phase where enzyme cuts the precursor protein. [NIH]

Enzyme: A protein that speeds up chemical reactions in the body. [NIH]

Epinephrine: The active sympathomimetic hormone from the adrenal medulla in most species. It stimulates both the alpha- and beta- adrenergic systems, causes systemic vasoconstriction and gastrointestinal relaxation, stimulates the heart, and dilates bronchi and cerebral vessels. It is used in asthma and cardiac failure and to delay absorption of local anesthetics. [NIH]

Esophagus: The muscular tube through which food passes from the throat to the stomach. [NIH]

Estrogen: One of the two female sex hormones. [NIH]

Estrogen receptor: ER. Protein found on some cancer cells to which estrogen will attach. [NIH]

Excitation: An act of irritation or stimulation or of responding to a stimulus; the addition of energy, as the excitation of a molecule by absorption of photons. [EU]

Exogenous: Developed or originating outside the organism, as exogenous disease. [EU]

Extracellular: Outside a cell or cells. [EU]

Extracellular Matrix: A meshwork-like substance found within the extracellular space and in association with the basement membrane of the cell surface. It promotes cellular proliferation and provides a supporting structure to which cells or cell lysates in culture dishes adhere. [NIH]

Extraction: The process or act of pulling or drawing out. [EU]

Extrapyramidal: Outside of the pyramidal tracts. [EU]

Family Planning: Programs or services designed to assist the family in controlling reproduction by either improving or diminishing fertility. [NIH]

Fat: Total lipids including phospholipids. [NIH]

Fatty acids: A major component of fats that are used by the body for energy and tissue development. [NIH]

Fertilization in Vitro: Fertilization of an egg outside the body when the egg is normally fertilized in the body. [NIH]

Fetus: The developing offspring from 7 to 8 weeks after conception until birth. [NIH]

Fibroblasts: Connective tissue cells which secrete an extracellular matrix rich in collagen and other macromolecules. [NIH]

Fibrosis: Any pathological condition where fibrous connective tissue invades any organ, usually as a consequence of inflammation or other injury. [NIH]

Fibrositis: Aching, soreness or stiffness of muscles; often caused by inexpedient work postures. [NIH]

Fissure: Any cleft or groove, normal or otherwise; especially a deep fold in the cerebral cortex which involves the entire thickness of the brain wall. [EU]

Fluorescence: The property of emitting radiation while being irradiated. The radiation emitted is usually of longer wavelength than that incident or absorbed, e.g., a substance can be irradiated with invisible radiation and emit visible light. X-ray fluorescence is used in diagnosis. [NIH]

Fluoxetine: The first highly specific serotonin uptake inhibitor. It is used as an antidepressant and often has a more acceptable side-effects profile than traditional antidepressants. [NIH]

Fold: A plication or doubling of various parts of the body. [NIH]

Free Association: Spontaneous verbalization of whatever comes to mind. [NIH]

Frontal Lobe: The anterior part of the cerebral hemisphere. [NIH]

Gallbladder: The pear-shaped organ that sits below the liver. Bile is concentrated and stored in the gallbladder. [NIH]

Ganglia: Clusters of multipolar neurons surrounded by a capsule of loosely organized connective tissue located outside the central nervous system. [NIH]

Gap Junctions: Connections between cells which allow passage of small molecules and electric current. Gap junctions were first described anatomically as regions of close apposition between cells with a narrow (1-2 nm) gap between cell membranes. The variety in the properties of gap junctions is reflected in the number of connexins, the family of proteins which form the junctions. [NIH]

Gas: Air that comes from normal breakdown of food. The gases are passed out of the body through the rectum (flatus) or the mouth (burp). [NIH]

Gastric: Having to do with the stomach. [NIH]

Gastrin: A hormone released after eating. Gastrin causes the stomach to produce more acid. [NIH]

Gastrointestinal: Refers to the stomach and intestines. [NIH]

Gastrointestinal tract: The stomach and intestines. [NIH]

Gene: The functional and physical unit of heredity passed from parent to offspring. Genes are pieces of DNA, and most genes contain the information for making a specific protein. [NIH]

Gene Expression: The phenotypic manifestation of a gene or genes by the processes of gene action. [NIH]

Genital: Pertaining to the genitalia. [EU]

Gestation: The period of development of the young in viviparous animals, from the time of fertilization of the ovum until birth. [EU]

Glucose: D-Glucose. A primary source of energy for living organisms. It is naturally occurring and is found in fruits and other parts of plants in its free state. It is used therapeutically in fluid and nutrient replacement. [NIH]

Glucose Intolerance: A pathological state in which the fasting plasma glucose level is less than 140 mg per deciliter and the 30-, 60-, or 90-minute plasma glucose concentration following a glucose tolerance test exceeds 200 mg per deciliter. This condition is seen frequently in diabetes mellitus but also occurs with other diseases. [NIH]

Glutamic Acid: A non-essential amino acid naturally occurring in the L-form. Glutamic acid (glutamate) is the most common excitatory neurotransmitter in the central nervous system. [NIH]

Glycine: A non-essential amino acid. It is found primarily in gelatin and silk fibroin and used therapeutically as a nutrient. It is also a fast inhibitory neurotransmitter. [NIH]

Glycoproteins: Conjugated protein-carbohydrate compounds including mucins, mucoid, and amyloid glycoproteins. [NIH]

Governing Board: The group in which legal authority is vested for the control of health-related institutions and organizations. [NIH]

Granulocytes: Leukocytes with abundant granules in the cytoplasm. They are divided into three groups: neutrophils, eosinophils, and basophils. [NIH]

Growth: The progressive development of a living being or part of an organism from its earliest stage to maturity. [NIH]

Happiness: Highly pleasant emotion characterized by outward manifestations of gratification; joy. [NIH]

Haptens: Small antigenic determinants capable of eliciting an immune response only when coupled to a carrier. Haptens bind to antibodies but by themselves cannot elicit an antibody response. [NIH]

Headache: Pain in the cranial region that may occur as an isolated and benign symptom or as a manifestation of a wide variety of conditions including subarachnoid hemorrhage; craniocerebral trauma; central nervous system infections; intracranial hypertension; and other disorders. In general, recurrent headaches that are not associated with a primary disease process are referred to as headache disorders (e.g., migraine). [NIH]

Hemorrhage: Bleeding or escape of blood from a vessel. [NIH]

Hemostasis: The process which spontaneously arrests the flow of blood from vessels carrying blood under pressure. It is accomplished by contraction of the vessels, adhesion and aggregation of formed blood elements, and the process of blood or plasma coagulation. [NIH]

Heredity: 1. The genetic transmission of a particular quality or trait from parent to offspring. 2. The genetic constitution of an individual. [EU]

Heterogeneity: The property of one or more samples or populations which implies that they are not identical in respect of some or all of their parameters, e. g. heterogeneity of variance. [NIH]

Homeostasis: The processes whereby the internal environment of an organism tends to remain balanced and stable. [NIH]

Homologous: Corresponding in structure, position, origin, etc., as (a) the feathers of a bird and the scales of a fish, (b) antigen and its specific antibody, (c) allelic chromosomes. [EU]

Hormonal: Pertaining to or of the nature of a hormone. [EU]

Hormone: A substance in the body that regulates certain organs. Hormones such as gastrin help in breaking down food. Some hormones come from cells in the stomach and small intestine. [NIH]

Hybridomas: Cells artificially created by fusion of activated lymphocytes with neoplastic cells. The resulting hybrid cells are cloned and produce pure or "monoclonal" antibodies or T-cell products, identical to those produced by the immunologically competent parent, and continually grow and divide as the neoplastic parent. [NIH]

Hydrogen: The first chemical element in the periodic table. It has the atomic symbol H, atomic number 1, and atomic weight 1. It exists, under normal conditions, as a colorless, odorless, tasteless, diatomic gas. Hydrogen ions are protons. Besides the common H1 isotope, hydrogen exists as the stable isotope deuterium and the unstable, radioactive isotope tritium. [NIH]

Hydrogen Bonding: A low-energy attractive force between hydrogen and another element. It plays a major role in determining the properties of water, proteins, and other compounds. [NIH]

Hydrogenation: Specific method of reduction in which hydrogen is added to a substance by the direct use of gaseous hydrogen. [NIH]

Hydroxyproline: A hydroxylated form of the imino acid proline. A deficiency in ascorbic acid can result in impaired hydroxyproline formation. [NIH]

Hypericum: Genus of perennial plants in the family Clusiaceae (Hypericaceae). Herbal and homeopathic preparations are used for depression, neuralgias, and a variety of other conditions. Contains flavonoids, glycosides, mucilage, tannins, and volatile oils (oils, essential). [NIH]

Hypersensitivity: Altered reactivity to an antigen, which can result in pathologic reactions upon subsequent exposure to that particular antigen. [NIH]

Hypertrophy: General increase in bulk of a part or organ, not due to tumor formation, nor to an increase in the number of cells. [NIH]

Hypnotic: A drug that acts to induce sleep. [EU]

Hypothalamic: Of or involving the hypothalamus. [EU]

Hypothalamus: Ventral part of the diencephalon extending from the region of the optic chiasm to the caudal border of the mammillary bodies and forming the inferior and lateral walls of the third ventricle. [NIH]

Id: The part of the personality structure which harbors the unconscious instinctive desires and strivings of the individual. [NIH]

Imipramine: The prototypical tricyclic antidepressant. It has been used in major depression, dysthymia, bipolar depression, attention-deficit disorders, agoraphobia, and panic disorders. It has less sedative effect than some other members of this therapeutic group. [NIH]

Immunology: The study of the body's immune system. [NIH]

Immunotherapy: Manipulation of the host's immune system in treatment of disease. It includes both active and passive immunization as well as immunosuppressive therapy to prevent graft rejection. [NIH]

Impairment: In the context of health experience, an impairment is any loss or abnormality of psychological, physiological, or anatomical structure or function. [NIH]

Impulse Control Disorders: Disorders whose essential features are the failure to resist an impulse, drive, or temptation to perform an act that is harmful to the individual or to others. Individuals experience an increased sense of tension prior to the act and pleasure, gratification, or release of tension at the time of committing the act. [NIH]

In vitro: In the laboratory (outside the body). The opposite of in vivo (in the body). [NIH]

In vivo: In the body. The opposite of in vitro (outside the body or in the laboratory). [NIH]

Indicative: That indicates; that points out more or less exactly; that reveals fairly clearly. [EU]

Infarction: A pathological process consisting of a sudden insufficient blood supply to an area, which results in necrosis of that area. It is usually caused by a thrombus, an embolus, or a vascular torsion. [NIH]

Infection: 1. Invasion and multiplication of microorganisms in body tissues, which may be clinically unapparent or result in local cellular injury due to competitive metabolism, toxins, intracellular replication, or antigen-antibody response. The infection may remain localized, subclinical, and temporary if the body's defensive mechanisms are effective. A local infection may persist and spread by extension to become an acute, subacute, or chronic clinical infection or disease state. A local infection may also become systemic when the microorganisms gain access to the lymphatic or vascular system. 2. An infectious disease. [EU]

Inflammation: A pathological process characterized by injury or destruction of tissues caused by a variety of cytologic and chemical reactions. It is usually manifested by typical signs of pain, heat, redness, swelling, and loss of function. [NIH]

Ingestion: Taking into the body by mouth [NIH]

Inhalation: The drawing of air or other substances into the lungs. [EU]

Inorganic: Pertaining to substances not of organic origin. [EU]

Inotropic: Affecting the force or energy of muscular contractions. [EU]

Insecticides: Pesticides designed to control insects that are harmful to man. The insects may be directly harmful, as those acting as disease vectors, or indirectly harmful, as destroyers of crops, food products, or textile fabrics. [NIH]

Insight: The capacity to understand one's own motives, to be aware of one's own psychodynamics, to appreciate the meaning of symbolic behavior. [NIH]

Insomnia: Difficulty in going to sleep or getting enough sleep. [NIH]

Interleukin-2: Chemical mediator produced by activated T lymphocytes and which regulates the proliferation of T cells, as well as playing a role in the regulation of NK cell activity. [NIH]

Interleukin-6: Factor that stimulates the growth and differentiation of human B-cells and is also a growth factor for hybridomas and plasmacytomas. It is produced by many different cells including T-cells, monocytes, and fibroblasts. [NIH]

Intracellular: Inside a cell. [NIH]

Intracellular Membranes: Membranes of subcellular structures. [NIH]

Intrinsic: Situated entirely within or pertaining exclusively to a part. [EU]

Ion Channels: Gated, ion-selective glycoproteins that traverse membranes. The stimulus for channel gating can be a membrane potential, drug, transmitter, cytoplasmic messenger, or a mechanical deformation. Ion channels which are integral parts of ionotropic neurotransmitter receptors are not included. [NIH]

Ions: An atom or group of atoms that have a positive or negative electric charge due to a gain (negative charge) or loss (positive charge) of one or more electrons. Atoms with a positive charge are known as cations; those with a negative charge are anions. [NIH]

Kb: A measure of the length of DNA fragments, 1 Kb = 1000 base pairs. The largest DNA fragments are up to 50 kilobases long. [NIH]

Kinetics: The study of rate dynamics in chemical or physical systems. [NIH]

Large Intestine: The part of the intestine that goes from the cecum to the rectum. The large intestine absorbs water from stool and changes it from a liquid to a solid form. The large intestine is 5 feet long and includes the appendix, cecum, colon, and rectum. Also called colon. [NIH]

Laterality: Behavioral manifestations of cerebral dominance in which there is preferential use and superior functioning of either the left or the right side, as in the preferred use of the right hand or right foot. [NIH]

Lectin: A complex molecule that has both protein and sugars. Lectins are able to bind to the outside of a cell and cause biochemical changes in it. Lectins are made by both animals and plants. [NIH]

Lethargy: Abnormal drowsiness or stupor; a condition of indifference. [EU]

Library Services: Services offered to the library user. They include reference and circulation. [NIH]

Limbic: Pertaining to a limbus, or margin; forming a border around. [EU]

Limbic System: A set of forebrain structures common to all mammals that is defined functionally and anatomically. It is implicated in the higher integration of visceral, olfactory, and somatic information as well as homeostatic responses including fundamental survival behaviors (feeding, mating, emotion). For most authors, it includes the amygdala, epithalamus, gyrus cinguli, hippocampal formation (see hippocampus), hypothalamus, parahippocampal gyrus, septal nuclei, anterior nuclear group of thalamus, and portions of the basal ganglia. (Parent, Carpenter's Human Neuroanatomy, 9th ed, p744; NeuroNames, http://rprcsgi.rprc.washington.edu/neuronames/index.html (September 2, 1998)). [NIH]

Liver: A large, glandular organ located in the upper abdomen. The liver cleanses the blood and aids in digestion by secreting bile. [NIH]

Localized: Cancer which has not metastasized yet. [NIH]

Locomotion: Movement or the ability to move from one place or another. It can refer to humans, vertebrate or invertebrate animals, and microorganisms. [NIH]

Lymphatic: The tissues and organs, including the bone marrow, spleen, thymus, and lymph nodes, that produce and store cells that fight infection and disease. [NIH]

Lymphocytes: White blood cells formed in the body's lymphoid tissue. The nucleus is round or ovoid with coarse, irregularly clumped chromatin while the cytoplasm is typically pale blue with azurophilic (if any) granules. Most lymphocytes can be classified as either T or B (with subpopulations of each); those with characteristics of neither major class are called null cells. [NIH]

Lymphoid: Referring to lymphocytes, a type of white blood cell. Also refers to tissue in which lymphocytes develop. [NIH]

Lymphoma: A general term for various neoplastic diseases of the lymphoid tissue. [NIH]

Mammary: Pertaining to the mamma, or breast. [EU]

Mandible: The largest and strongest bone of the face constituting the lower jaw. It supports the lower teeth. [NIH]

Mediate: Indirect; accomplished by the aid of an intervening medium. [EU]

Mediator: An object or substance by which something is mediated, such as (1) a structure of the nervous system that transmits impulses eliciting a specific response; (2) a chemical substance (transmitter substance) that induces activity in an excitable tissue, such as nerve or muscle; or (3) a substance released from cells as the result of the interaction of antigen with antibody or by the action of antigen with a sensitized lymphocyte. [EU]

MEDLINE: An online database of MEDLARS, the computerized bibliographic Medical Literature Analysis and Retrieval System of the National Library of Medicine. [NIH]

Meiosis: A special method of cell division, occurring in maturation of the germ cells, by means of which each daughter nucleus receives half the number of chromosomes characteristic of the somatic cells of the species. [NIH]

Membrane: A very thin layer of tissue that covers a surface. [NIH]

Membrane Proteins: Proteins which are found in membranes including cellular and intracellular membranes. They consist of two types, peripheral and integral proteins. They include most membrane-associated enzymes, antigenic proteins, transport proteins, and drug, hormone, and lectin receptors. [NIH]

Memory: Complex mental function having four distinct phases: (1) memorizing or learning, (2) retention, (3) recall, and (4) recognition. Clinically, it is usually subdivided into immediate, recent, and remote memory. [NIH]

Menopause: Permanent cessation of menstruation. [NIH]

Menstrual Cycle: The period of the regularly recurring physiologic changes in the endometrium occurring during the reproductive period in human females and some primates and culminating in partial sloughing of the endometrium (menstruation). [NIH]

Menstruation: The normal physiologic discharge through the vagina of blood and mucosal tissues from the nonpregnant uterus. [NIH]

Mental: Pertaining to the mind; psychic. 2. (L. mentum chin) pertaining to the chin. [EU]

Mental Disorders: Psychiatric illness or diseases manifested by breakdowns in the adaptational process expressed primarily as abnormalities of thought, feeling, and behavior producing either distress or impairment of function. [NIH]

Mental Health: The state wherein the person is well adjusted. [NIH]

Mental Processes: Conceptual functions or thinking in all its forms. [NIH]

Methamphetamine: A central nervous system stimulant and sympathomimetic with actions and uses similar to dextroamphetamine. The smokable form is a drug of abuse and is referred to as crank, crystal, crystal meth, ice, and speed. [NIH]

Methanol: A colorless, flammable liquid used in the manufacture of formaldehyde and acetic acid, in chemical synthesis, antifreeze, and as a solvent. Ingestion of methanol is toxic and may cause blindness. [NIH]

Methylphenidate: A central nervous system stimulant used most commonly in the treatment of attention-deficit disorders in children and for narcolepsy. Its mechanisms appear to be similar to those of dextroamphetamine. [NIH]

MI: Myocardial infarction. Gross necrosis of the myocardium as a result of interruption of the blood supply to the area; it is almost always caused by atherosclerosis of the coronary arteries, upon which coronary thrombosis is usually superimposed. [NIH]

Microbe: An organism which cannot be observed with the naked eye; e. g. unicellular animals, lower algae, lower fungi, bacteria. [NIH]

Microbiology: The study of microorganisms such as fungi, bacteria, algae, archaea, and viruses. [NIH]

Microglia: The third type of glial cell, along with astrocytes and oligodendrocytes (which together form the macroglia). Microglia vary in appearance depending on developmental stage, functional state, and anatomical location; subtype terms include ramified, perivascular, ameboid, resting, and activated. Microglia clearly are capable of phagocytosis and play an important role in a wide spectrum of neuropathologies. They have also been suggested to act in several other roles including in secretion (e.g., of cytokines and neural growth factors), in immunological processing (e.g., antigen presentation), and in central nervous system development and remodeling. [NIH]

Modification: A change in an organism, or in a process in an organism, that is acquired from its own activity or environment. [NIH]

Molecular: Of, pertaining to, or composed of molecules : a very small mass of matter. [EU]

Molecular Structure: The location of the atoms, groups or ions relative to one another in a molecule, as well as the number, type and location of covalent bonds. [NIH]

Molecule: A chemical made up of two or more atoms. The atoms in a molecule can be the same (an oxygen molecule has two oxygen atoms) or different (a water molecule has two hydrogen atoms and one oxygen atom). Biological molecules, such as proteins and DNA, can be made up of many thousands of atoms. [NIH]

Monoamine: Enzyme that breaks down dopamine in the astrocytes and microglia. [NIH]

Monoamine Oxidase: An enzyme that catalyzes the oxidative deamination of naturally occurring monoamines. It is a flavin-containing enzyme that is localized in mitochondrial membranes, whether in nerve terminals, the liver, or other organs. Monoamine oxidase is important in regulating the metabolic degradation of catecholamines and serotonin in neural or target tissues. Hepatic monoamine oxidase has a crucial defensive role in inactivating circulating monoamines or those, such as tyramine, that originate in the gut and are absorbed into the portal circulation. (From Goodman and Gilman's, The Pharmacological Basis of Therapeutics, 8th ed, p415) EC 1.4.3.4. [NIH]

Monocytes: Large, phagocytic mononuclear leukocytes produced in the vertebrate bone marrow and released into the blood; contain a large, oval or somewhat indented nucleus surrounded by voluminous cytoplasm and numerous organelles. [NIH]

Mood Disorders: Those disorders that have a disturbance in mood as their predominant feature. [NIH]

Morphogenesis: The development of the form of an organ, part of the body, or organism. [NIH]

Motility: The ability to move spontaneously. [EU]

Muscle Relaxation: That phase of a muscle twitch during which a muscle returns to a resting position. [NIH]

Musculature: The muscular apparatus of the body, or of any part of it. [EU]

Myocardium: The muscle tissue of the heart composed of striated, involuntary muscle known as cardiac muscle. [NIH]

Naloxone: A specific opiate antagonist that has no agonist activity. It is a competitive antagonist at mu, delta, and kappa opioid receptors. [NIH]

Narcolepsy: A condition of unknown cause characterized by a periodic uncontrollable tendency to fall asleep. [NIH]

Nausea: An unpleasant sensation in the stomach usually accompanied by the urge to vomit. Common causes are early pregnancy, sea and motion sickness, emotional stress, intense pain, food poisoning, and various enteroviruses. [NIH]

NCI: National Cancer Institute. NCI, part of the National Institutes of Health of the United States Department of Health and Human Services, is the federal government's principal agency for cancer research. NCI conducts, coordinates, and funds cancer research, training, health information dissemination, and other programs with respect to the cause, diagnosis, prevention, and treatment of cancer. Access the NCI Web site at http://cancer.gov. [NIH]

Need: A state of tension or dissatisfaction felt by an individual that impels him to action toward a goal he believes will satisfy the impulse. [NIH]

Neoplastic: Pertaining to or like a neoplasm (= any new and abnormal growth); pertaining to neoplasia (= the formation of a neoplasm). [EU]

Nerve: A cordlike structure of nervous tissue that connects parts of the nervous system with other tissues of the body and conveys nervous impulses to, or away from, these tissues. [NIH]

Nervous System: The entire nerve apparatus composed of the brain, spinal cord, nerves and ganglia. [NIH]

Neural: 1. Pertaining to a nerve or to the nerves. 2. Situated in the region of the spinal axis, as the neutral arch. [EU]

Neuroendocrine: Having to do with the interactions between the nervous system and the endocrine system. Describes certain cells that release hormones into the blood in response to stimulation of the nervous system. [NIH]

Neuromuscular: Pertaining to muscles and nerves. [EU]

Neuromuscular Junction: The synapse between a neuron and a muscle. [NIH]

Neuronal: Pertaining to a neuron or neurons (= conducting cells of the nervous system). [EU]

Neurons: The basic cellular units of nervous tissue. Each neuron consists of a body, an axon, and dendrites. Their purpose is to receive, conduct, and transmit impulses in the nervous system. [NIH]

Neuropeptide: A member of a class of protein-like molecules made in the brain. Neuropeptides consist of short chains of amino acids, with some functioning as neurotransmitters and some functioning as hormones. [NIH]

Neuropharmacology: The branch of pharmacology dealing especially with the action of drugs upon various parts of the nervous system. [NIH]

Neurotoxic: Poisonous or destructive to nerve tissue. [EU]

Neurotransmitter: Any of a group of substances that are released on excitation from the axon terminal of a presynaptic neuron of the central or peripheral nervous system and travel across the synaptic cleft to either excite or inhibit the target cell. Among the many substances that have the properties of a neurotransmitter are acetylcholine, norepinephrine, epinephrine, dopamine, glycine, y-aminobutyrate, glutamic acid, substance P, enkephalins, endorphins, and serotonin. [EU]

Nitrazepam: A benzodiazepine derivative used as an anticonvulsant and hypnotic. [NIH]

Nitrogen: An element with the atomic symbol N, atomic number 7, and atomic weight 14. Nitrogen exists as a diatomic gas and makes up about 78% of the earth's atmosphere by volume. It is a constituent of proteins and nucleic acids and found in all living cells. [NIH]

Nonverbal Communication: Transmission of emotions, ideas, and attitudes between individuals in ways other than the spoken language. [NIH]

Norepinephrine: Precursor of epinephrine that is secreted by the adrenal medulla and is a widespread central and autonomic neurotransmitter. Norepinephrine is the principal transmitter of most postganglionic sympathetic fibers and of the diffuse projection system in the brain arising from the locus ceruleus. It is also found in plants and is used pharmacologically as a sympathomimetic. [NIH]

Nuclei: A body of specialized protoplasm found in nearly all cells and containing the chromosomes. [NIH]

Nucleic acid: Either of two types of macromolecule (DNA or RNA) formed by polymerization of nucleotides. Nucleic acids are found in all living cells and contain the information (genetic code) for the transfer of genetic information from one generation to the next. [NIH]

Obsessive-Compulsive Disorder: An anxiety disorder characterized by recurrent, persistent obsessions or compulsions. Obsessions are the intrusive ideas, thoughts, or images that are experienced as senseless or repugnant. Compulsions are repetitive and seemingly purposeful behavior which the individual generally recognizes as senseless and from which the individual does not derive pleasure although it may provide a release from tension. [NIH]

Octanes: Eight-carbon saturated hydrocarbon group of the methane series. Include isomers and derivatives. [NIH]

Odour: A volatile emanation that is perceived by the sense of smell. [EU]

Opiate: A remedy containing or derived from opium; also any drug that induces sleep. [EU]

Optic Chiasm: The X-shaped structure formed by the meeting of the two optic nerves. At the optic chiasm the fibers from the medial part of each retina cross to project to the other side of the brain while the lateral retinal fibers continue on the same side. As a result each half of the brain receives information about the contralateral visual field from both eyes. [NIH]

Osteoclasts: A large multinuclear cell associated with the absorption and removal of bone. An odontoclast, also called cementoclast, is cytomorphologically the same as an osteoclast and is involved in cementum resorption. [NIH]

Overdose: An accidental or deliberate dose of a medication or street drug that is in excess of what is normally used. [NIH]

Ovum: A female germ cell extruded from the ovary at ovulation. [NIH]

Pancreas: A mixed exocrine and endocrine gland situated transversely across the posterior abdominal wall in the epigastric and hypochondriac regions. The endocrine portion is comprised of the Islets of Langerhans, while the exocrine portion is a compound acinar gland that secretes digestive enzymes. [NIH]

Panic: A state of extreme acute, intense anxiety and unreasoning fear accompanied by disorganization of personality function. [NIH]

Panic Disorder: A type of anxiety disorder characterized by unexpected panic attacks that last minutes or, rarely, hours. Panic attacks begin with intense apprehension, fear or terror and, often, a feeling of impending doom. Symptoms experienced during a panic attack include dyspnea or sensations of being smothered; dizziness, loss of balance or faintness; choking sensations; palpitations or accelerated heart rate; shakiness; sweating; nausea or other form of abdominal distress; depersonalization or derealization; paresthesias; hot flashes or chills; chest discomfort or pain; fear of dying and fear of not being in control of oneself or going crazy. Agoraphobia may also develop. Similar to other anxiety disorders, it may be inherited as an autosomal dominant trait. [NIH]

Paresthesias: Abnormal touch sensations, such as burning or prickling, that occur without an outside stimulus. [NIH]

Pathologic: 1. Indicative of or caused by a morbid condition. 2. Pertaining to pathology (= branch of medicine that treats the essential nature of the disease, especially the structural and functional changes in tissues and organs of the body caused by the disease). [EU]

Peptide: Any compound consisting of two or more amino acids, the building blocks of proteins. Peptides are combined to make proteins. [NIH]

Perennial: Lasting through the year of for several years. [EU]

Perfusion: Bathing an organ or tissue with a fluid. In regional perfusion, a specific area of the body (usually an arm or a leg) receives high doses of anticancer drugs through a blood vessel. Such a procedure is performed to treat cancer that has not spread. [NIH]

Peripheral Nervous System: The nervous system outside of the brain and spinal cord. The peripheral nervous system has autonomic and somatic divisions. The autonomic nervous system includes the enteric, parasympathetic, and sympathetic subdivisions. The somatic nervous system includes the cranial and spinal nerves and their ganglia and the peripheral sensory receptors. [NIH]

Pesticides: Chemicals used to destroy pests of any sort. The concept includes fungicides (industrial fungicides), insecticides, rodenticides, etc. [NIH]

Pharmacologic: Pertaining to pharmacology or to the properties and reactions of drugs. [EU]

Pharmacotherapy: A regimen of using appetite suppressant medications to manage obesity by decreasing appetite or increasing the feeling of satiety. These medications decrease appetite by increasing serotonin or catecholamine—two brain chemicals that affect mood and appetite. [NIH]

Phospholipases: A class of enzymes that catalyze the hydrolysis of phosphoglycerides or glycerophosphatidates. EC 3.1.-. [NIH]

Physiologic: Having to do with the functions of the body. When used in the phrase "physiologic age," it refers to an age assigned by general health, as opposed to calendar age. [NIH]

Placebos: Any dummy medication or treatment. Although placebos originally were medicinal preparations having no specific pharmacological activity against a targeted condition, the concept has been extended to include treatments or procedures, especially those administered to control groups in clinical trials in order to provide baseline measurements for the experimental protocol. [NIH]

Placenta: A highly vascular fetal organ through which the fetus absorbs oxygen and other nutrients and excretes carbon dioxide and other wastes. It begins to form about the eighth day of gestation when the blastocyst adheres to the decidua. [NIH]

Plants: Multicellular, eukaryotic life forms of the kingdom Plantae. They are characterized by a mainly photosynthetic mode of nutrition; essentially unlimited growth at localized regions of cell divisions (meristems); cellulose within cells providing rigidity; the absence of organs of locomotion; absense of nervous and sensory systems; and an alteration of haploid and diploid generations. [NIH]

Plasma: The clear, yellowish, fluid part of the blood that carries the blood cells. The proteins that form blood clots are in plasma. [NIH]

Plasticity: In an individual or a population, the capacity for adaptation: a) through gene changes (genetic plasticity) or b) through internal physiological modifications in response to changes of environment (physiological plasticity). [NIH]

Platelet Activation: A series of progressive, overlapping events triggered by exposure of the platelets to subendothelial tissue. These events include shape change, adhesiveness, aggregation, and release reactions. When carried through to completion, these events lead to the formation of a stable hemostatic plug. [NIH]

Pneumonia: Inflammation of the lungs. [NIH]

Poisoning: A condition or physical state produced by the ingestion, injection or inhalation of, or exposure to a deleterious agent. [NIH]

Posterior: Situated in back of, or in the back part of, or affecting the back or dorsal surface of the body. In lower animals, it refers to the caudal end of the body. [EU]

Postmenopausal: Refers to the time after menopause. Menopause is the time in a woman's life when menstrual periods stop permanently; also called "change of life." [NIH]

Postsynaptic: Nerve potential generated by an inhibitory hyperpolarizing stimulation. [NIH]

Post-traumatic: Occurring as a result of or after injury. [EU]

Post-traumatic stress disorder: A psychological disorder that develops in some individuals after a major traumatic experience such as war, rape, domestic violence, or accident. [NIH]

Potassium: An element that is in the alkali group of metals. It has an atomic symbol K, atomic number 19, and atomic weight 39.10. It is the chief cation in the intracellular fluid of muscle and other cells. Potassium ion is a strong electrolyte and it plays a significant role in the regulation of fluid volume and maintenance of the water-electrolyte balance. [NIH]

Potentiates: A degree of synergism which causes the exposure of the organism to a harmful substance to worsen a disease already contracted. [NIH]

Potentiation: An overall effect of two drugs taken together which is greater than the sum of the effects of each drug taken alone. [NIH]

Practice Guidelines: Directions or principles presenting current or future rules of policy for the health care practitioner to assist him in patient care decisions regarding diagnosis, therapy, or related clinical circumstances. The guidelines may be developed by government agencies at any level, institutions, professional societies, governing boards, or by the convening of expert panels. The guidelines form a basis for the evaluation of all aspects of health care and delivery. [NIH]

Preclinical: Before a disease becomes clinically recognizable. [EU]

Precursor: Something that precedes. In biological processes, a substance from which another, usually more active or mature substance is formed. In clinical medicine, a sign or symptom that heralds another. [EU]

Pregnancy Outcome: Results of conception and ensuing pregnancy, including live birth, stillbirth, spontaneous abortion, induced abortion. The outcome may follow natural or artificial insemination or any of the various reproduction techniques, such as embryo transfer or fertilization in vitro. [NIH]

Premenstrual: Occurring before menstruation. [EU]

Premenstrual Syndrome: A syndrome occurring most often during the last week of the menstrual cycle and ending soon after the onset of menses. Some of the symptoms are emotional instability, insomnia, headache, nausea, vomiting, abdominal distension, and painful breasts. [NIH]

Prenatal: Existing or occurring before birth, with reference to the fetus. [EU]

Presynaptic: Situated proximal to a synapse, or occurring before the synapse is crossed. [EU]

Progesterone: Pregn-4-ene-3,20-dione. The principal progestational hormone of the body, secreted by the corpus luteum, adrenal cortex, and placenta. Its chief function is to prepare the uterus for the reception and development of the fertilized ovum. It acts as an antiovulatory agent when administered on days 5-25 of the menstrual cycle. [NIH]

Progression: Increase in the size of a tumor or spread of cancer in the body. [NIH]

Progressive: Advancing; going forward; going from bad to worse; increasing in scope or severity. [EU]

Projection: A defense mechanism, operating unconsciously, whereby that which is emotionally unacceptable in the self is rejected and attributed (projected) to others. [NIH]

Prone: Having the front portion of the body downwards. [NIH]

Prophase: The first phase of cell division, in which the chromosomes become visible, the nucleus starts to lose its identity, the spindle appears, and the centrioles migrate toward opposite poles. [NIH]

Prostaglandins: A group of compounds derived from unsaturated 20-carbon fatty acids, primarily arachidonic acid, via the cyclooxygenase pathway. They are extremely potent mediators of a diverse group of physiological processes. [NIH]

Protein S: The vitamin K-dependent cofactor of activated protein C. Together with protein C, it inhibits the action of factors VIIIa and Va. A deficiency in protein S can lead to recurrent venous and arterial thrombosis. [NIH]

Proteins: Polymers of amino acids linked by peptide bonds. The specific sequence of amino acids determines the shape and function of the protein. [NIH]

Protocol: The detailed plan for a clinical trial that states the trial's rationale, purpose, drug or vaccine dosages, length of study, routes of administration, who may participate, and other aspects of trial design. [NIH]

Protons: Stable elementary particles having the smallest known positive charge, found in the nuclei of all elements. The proton mass is less than that of a neutron. A proton is the nucleus of the light hydrogen atom, i.e., the hydrogen ion. [NIH]

Prozac: Antidepressant of the SSRI class. [NIH]

Pseudoxanthoma: A rare disease of the skin characterized by the appearance of elevated yellowish papules or plaques, particularly on the neck, chest an abdomen and infrequently on the eyelids. [NIH]

Pseudoxanthoma Elasticum: A rare, progressive inherited disorder resulting from extensive basophilic degeneration of elastic tissue, usually presenting after puberty and involving the skin, eye, and cardiovascular system. Characteristic manifestations are small, circumscribed yellowish patches at sites of considerable movement of the skin, angioid streaks in the retina, and a tendency towards hemorrhage and arterial insufficiency. [NIH]

Psychiatric: Pertaining to or within the purview of psychiatry. [EU]

Psychiatry: The medical science that deals with the origin, diagnosis, prevention, and treatment of mental disorders. [NIH]

Psychic: Pertaining to the psyche or to the mind; mental. [EU]

Psychoactive: Those drugs which alter sensation, mood, consciousness or other psychological or behavioral functions. [NIH]

Psychoanalysis: The separation or resolution of the psyche into its constituent elements. The term has two separate meanings: 1. a procedure devised by Sigmund Freud, for investigating mental processes by means of free association, dream interpretation and interpretation of resistance and transference manifestations; and 2. a theory of psychology developed by Freud from his clinical experience with hysterical patients. (From Campbell, Psychiatric Dictionary, 1996). [NIH]

Psychology: The science dealing with the study of mental processes and behavior in man and animals. [NIH]

Psychotherapy: A generic term for the treatment of mental illness or emotional disturbances primarily by verbal or nonverbal communication. [NIH]

Psychotropic: Exerting an effect upon the mind; capable of modifying mental activity; usually applied to drugs that effect the mental state. [EU]

Puberty: The period during which the secondary sex characteristics begin to develop and the capability of sexual reproduction is attained. [EU]

Public Policy: A course or method of action selected, usually by a government, from among alternatives to guide and determine present and future decisions. [NIH]

Pulmonary: Relating to the lungs. [NIH]

Pulmonary hypertension: Abnormally high blood pressure in the arteries of the lungs. [NIH]

Radiation: Emission or propagation of electromagnetic energy (waves/rays), or the waves/rays themselves; a stream of electromagnetic particles (electrons, neutrons, protons, alpha particles) or a mixture of these. The most common source is the sun. [NIH]

Radioactive: Giving off radiation. [NIH]

Randomized: Describes an experiment or clinical trial in which animal or human subjects are assigned by chance to separate groups that compare different treatments. [NIH]

Rape: Unlawful sexual intercourse without consent of the victim. [NIH]

Receptor: A molecule inside or on the surface of a cell that binds to a specific substance and causes a specific physiologic effect in the cell. [NIH]

Receptors, Serotonin: Cell-surface proteins that bind serotonin and trigger intracellular changes which influence the behavior of cells. Several types of serotonin receptors have been recognized which differ in their pharmacology, molecular biology, and mode of action. [NIH]

Rectum: The last 8 to 10 inches of the large intestine. [NIH]

Refer: To send or direct for treatment, aid, information, de decision. [NIH]

Regimen: A treatment plan that specifies the dosage, the schedule, and the duration of treatment. [NIH]

Regression Analysis: Procedures for finding the mathematical function which best describes the relationship between a dependent variable and one or more independent variables. In linear regression (see linear models) the relationship is constrained to be a straight line and least-squares analysis is used to determine the best fit. In logistic regression (see logistic models) the dependent variable is qualitative rather than continuously variable and likelihood functions are used to find the best relationship. In multiple regression the dependent variable is considered to depend on more than a single independent variable. [NIH]

Reproduction Techniques: Methods pertaining to the generation of new individuals. [NIH]

Resorption: The loss of substance through physiologic or pathologic means, such as loss of dentin and cementum of a tooth, or of the alveolar process of the mandible or maxilla. [EU]

Respiration: The act of breathing with the lungs, consisting of inspiration, or the taking into the lungs of the ambient air, and of expiration, or the expelling of the modified air which contains more carbon dioxide than the air taken in (Blakiston's Gould Medical Dictionary, 4th ed.). This does not include tissue respiration (= oxygen consumption) or cell respiration (= cell respiration). [NIH]

Retina: The ten-layered nervous tissue membrane of the eye. It is continuous with the optic nerve and receives images of external objects and transmits visual impulses to the brain. Its outer surface is in contact with the choroid and the inner surface with the vitreous body. The outer-most layer is pigmented, whereas the inner nine layers are transparent. [NIH]

Rodenticides: Substances used to destroy or inhibit the action of rats, mice, or other rodents. [NIH]

Salivary: The duct that convey saliva to the mouth. [NIH]

Salivary glands: Glands in the mouth that produce saliva. [NIH]

Screening: Checking for disease when there are no symptoms. [NIH]

Secretory: Secreting; relating to or influencing secretion or the secretions. [NIH]

Sedative: 1. Allaying activity and excitement. 2. An agent that allays excitement. [EU]

Seizures: Clinical or subclinical disturbances of cortical function due to a sudden, abnormal, excessive, and disorganized discharge of brain cells. Clinical manifestations include abnormal motor, sensory and psychic phenomena. Recurrent seizures are usually referred to as epilepsy or "seizure disorder." [NIH]

Selective estrogen receptor modulator: SERM. A drug that acts like estrogen on some tissues, but blocks the effect of estrogen on other tissues. Tamoxifen and raloxifene are SERMs. [NIH]

Serotonin: A biochemical messenger and regulator, synthesized from the essential amino acid L-tryptophan. In humans it is found primarily in the central nervous system, gastrointestinal tract, and blood platelets. Serotonin mediates several important physiological functions including neurotransmission, gastrointestinal motility, hemostasis, and cardiovascular integrity. Multiple receptor families (receptors, serotonin) explain the broad physiological actions and distribution of this biochemical mediator. [NIH]

Serotonin Uptake Inhibitors: Compounds that specifically inhibit the reuptake of serotonin in the brain. This increases the serotonin concentration in the synaptic cleft which then activates serotonin receptors to a greater extent. These agents have been used in treatment of depression, panic disorder, obsessive-compulsive behavior, and alcoholism, as analgesics, and to treat obesity and bulimia. Many of the adrenergic uptake inhibitors also inhibit serotonin uptake; they are not included here. [NIH]

Sertraline: A selective serotonin uptake inhibitor that is used in the treatment of depression. [NIH]

Sibutramine: A drug used for the management of obesity that helps reduce food intake and is indicated for weight loss and maintenance of weight loss when used in conjunction with a reduced-calorie diet. It works to suppress the appetite primarily by inhibiting the reuptake of the neurotransmitters norepinephrine and serotonin. Side effects include dry mouth, headache, constipation, insomnia, and a slight increase in average blood pressure. In some patients it causes a higher blood pressure increase. [NIH]

Side effect: A consequence other than the one(s) for which an agent or measure is used, as the adverse effects produced by a drug, especially on a tissue or organ system other than the one sought to be benefited by its administration. [EU]

Signal Transduction: The intercellular or intracellular transfer of information (biological activation/inhibition) through a signal pathway. In each signal transduction system, an activation/inhibition signal from a biologically active molecule (hormone, neurotransmitter) is mediated via the coupling of a receptor/enzyme to a second messenger system or to an ion channel. Signal transduction plays an important role in activating cellular functions, cell differentiation, and cell proliferation. Examples of signal transduction systems are the GABA-postsynaptic receptor-calcium ion channel system, the receptor-mediated T-cell activation pathway, and the receptor-mediated activation of phospholipases. Those coupled to membrane depolarization or intracellular release of calcium include the receptor-mediated activation of cytotoxic functions in granulocytes and the synaptic potentiation of protein kinase activation. Some signal transduction pathways may be part of larger signal transduction pathways; for example, protein kinase activation is part of the platelet activation signal pathway. [NIH]

Silicon: A trace element that constitutes about 27.6% of the earth's crust in the form of silicon dioxide. It does not occur free in nature. Silicon has the atomic symbol Si, atomic number 14, and atomic weight 28.09. [NIH]

Silicon Dioxide: Silica. Transparent, tasteless crystals found in nature as agate, amethyst, chalcedony, cristobalite, flint, sand, quartz, and tridymite. The compound is insoluble in water or acids except hydrofluoric acid. [NIH]

Skeletal: Having to do with the skeleton (boney part of the body). [NIH]

Skeleton: The framework that supports the soft tissues of vertebrate animals and protects many of their internal organs. The skeletons of vertebrates are made of bone and/or cartilage. [NIH]

Small intestine: The part of the digestive tract that is located between the stomach and the large intestine. [NIH]

Smoking Cessation: Discontinuation of the habit of smoking, the inhaling and exhaling of tobacco smoke. [NIH]

Social Work: The use of community resources, individual case work, or group work to promote the adaptive capacities of individuals in relation to their social and economic environments. It includes social service agencies. [NIH]

Solvent: 1. Dissolving; effecting a solution. 2. A liquid that dissolves or that is capable of dissolving; the component of a solution that is present in greater amount. [EU]

Specialist: In medicine, one who concentrates on 1 special branch of medical science. [NIH]

Specificity: Degree of selectivity shown by an antibody with respect to the number and types of antigens with which the antibody combines, as well as with respect to the rates and the extents of these reactions. [NIH]

Spontaneous Abortion: The non-induced birth of an embryo or of fetus prior to the stage of viability at about 20 weeks of gestation. [NIH]

Steroid: A group name for lipids that contain a hydrogenated cyclopentanoperhydrophenanthrene ring system. Some of the substances included in this group are progesterone, adrenocortical hormones, the gonadal hormones, cardiac aglycones, bile acids, sterols (such as cholesterol), toad poisons, saponins, and some of the carcinogenic hydrocarbons. [EU]

Stillbirth: The birth of a dead fetus or baby. [NIH]

Stimulant: 1. Producing stimulation; especially producing stimulation by causing tension on muscle fibre through the nervous tissue. 2. An agent or remedy that produces stimulation. [EU]

Stimulus: That which can elicit or evoke action (response) in a muscle, nerve, gland or other excitable issue, or cause an augmenting action upon any function or metabolic process. [NIH]

Stomach: An organ of digestion situated in the left upper quadrant of the abdomen between the termination of the esophagus and the beginning of the duodenum. [NIH]

Stress: Forcibly exerted influence; pressure. Any condition or situation that causes strain or tension. Stress may be either physical or psychologic, or both. [NIH]

Striatum: A higher brain's domain thus called because of its stripes. [NIH]

Stroke: Sudden loss of function of part of the brain because of loss of blood flow. Stroke may be caused by a clot (thrombosis) or rupture (hemorrhage) of a blood vessel to the brain. [NIH]

Stupor: Partial or nearly complete unconsciousness, manifested by the subject's responding only to vigorous stimulation. Also, in psychiatry, a disorder marked by reduced responsiveness. [EU]

Subacute: Somewhat acute; between acute and chronic. [EU]

Subclinical: Without clinical manifestations; said of the early stage(s) of an infection or other disease or abnormality before symptoms and signs become apparent or detectable by clinical examination or laboratory tests, or of a very mild form of an infection or other disease or abnormality. [EU]

Substrate: A substance upon which an enzyme acts. [EU]

Supplementation: Adding nutrients to the diet. [NIH]

Sympathomimetic: 1. Mimicking the effects of impulses conveyed by adrenergic postganglionic fibres of the sympathetic nervous system. 2. An agent that produces effects similar to those of impulses conveyed by adrenergic postganglionic fibres of the sympathetic nervous system. Called also adrenergic. [EU]

Synapse: The region where the processes of two neurons come into close contiguity, and the nervous impulse passes from one to the other; the fibers of the two are intermeshed, but, according to the general view, there is no direct contiguity. [NIH]

Synapsis: The pairing between homologous chromosomes of maternal and paternal origin during the prophase of meiosis, leading to the formation of gametes. [NIH]

Synaptic: Pertaining to or affecting a synapse (= site of functional apposition between neurons, at which an impulse is transmitted from one neuron to another by electrical or chemical means); pertaining to synapsis (= pairing off in point-for-point association of homologous chromosomes from the male and female pronuclei during the early prophase of meiosis). [EU]

Synaptic Transmission: The communication from a neuron to a target (neuron, muscle, or secretory cell) across a synapse. In chemical synaptic transmission, the presynaptic neuron releases a neurotransmitter that diffuses across the synaptic cleft and binds to specific synaptic receptors. These activated receptors modulate ion channels and/or second-messenger systems to influence the postsynaptic cell. Electrical transmission is less common in the nervous system, and, as in other tissues, is mediated by gap junctions. [NIH]

Synaptic Vesicles: Membrane-bound compartments which contain transmitter molecules. Synaptic vesicles are concentrated at presynaptic terminals. They actively sequester transmitter molecules from the cytoplasm. In at least some synapses, transmitter release occurs by fusion of these vesicles with the presynaptic membrane, followed by exocytosis of their contents. [NIH]

Systemic: Affecting the entire body. [NIH]

Tachycardia: Excessive rapidity in the action of the heart, usually with a heart rate above 100 beats per minute. [NIH]

Tamoxifen: A first generation selective estrogen receptor modulator (SERM). It acts as an agonist for bone tissue and cholesterol metabolism but is an estrogen antagonist in mammary and uterine. [NIH]

Temporal: One of the two irregular bones forming part of the lateral surfaces and base of the skull, and containing the organs of hearing. [NIH]

Temporal Lobe: Lower lateral part of the cerebral hemisphere. [NIH]

Third Ventricle: A narrow cleft inferior to the corpus callosum, within the diencephalon, between the paired thalami. Its floor is formed by the hypothalamus, its anterior wall by the lamina terminalis, and its roof by ependyma. It communicates with the fourth ventricle by the cerebral aqueduct, and with the lateral ventricles by the interventricular foramina. [NIH]

Thrombosis: The formation or presence of a blood clot inside a blood vessel. [NIH]

Tissue: A group or layer of cells that are alike in type and work together to perform a specific function. [NIH]

Tolerance: 1. The ability to endure unusually large doses of a drug or toxin. 2. Acquired drug tolerance; a decreasing response to repeated constant doses of a drug or the need for increasing doses to maintain a constant response. [EU]

Tomography: Imaging methods that result in sharp images of objects located on a chosen plane and blurred images located above or below the plane. [NIH]

Tone: 1. The normal degree of vigour and tension; in muscle, the resistance to passive elongation or stretch; tonus. 2. A particular quality of sound or of voice. 3. To make permanent, or to change, the colour of silver stain by chemical treatment, usually with a heavy metal. [EU]

Tonic: 1. Producing and restoring the normal tone. 2. Characterized by continuous tension. 3. A term formerly used for a class of medicinal preparations believed to have the power of restoring normal tone to tissue. [EU]

Tooth Preparation: Procedures carried out with regard to the teeth or tooth structures preparatory to specified dental therapeutic and surgical measures. [NIH]

Torture: The intentional infliction of physical or mental suffering upon an individual or individuals, including the torture of animals. [NIH]

Toxic: Having to do with poison or something harmful to the body. Toxic substances usually cause unwanted side effects. [NIH]

Toxicity: The quality of being poisonous, especially the degree of virulence of a toxic microbe or of a poison. [EU]

Toxicology: The science concerned with the detection, chemical composition, and pharmacologic action of toxic substances or poisons and the treatment and prevention of toxic manifestations. [NIH]

Toxin: A poison; frequently used to refer specifically to a protein produced by some higher plants, certain animals, and pathogenic bacteria, which is highly toxic for other living organisms. Such substances are differentiated from the simple chemical poisons and the vegetable alkaloids by their high molecular weight and antigenicity. [EU]

Trace element: Substance or element essential to plant or animal life, but present in extremely small amounts. [NIH]

Transduction: The transfer of genes from one cell to another by means of a viral (in the case of bacteria, a bacteriophage) vector or a vector which is similar to a virus particle (pseudovirion). [NIH]

Transfection: The uptake of naked or purified DNA into cells, usually eukaryotic. It is analogous to bacterial transformation. [NIH]

Translation: The process whereby the genetic information present in the linear sequence of ribonucleotides in mRNA is converted into a corresponding sequence of amino acids in a protein. It occurs on the ribosome and is unidirectional. [NIH]

Translocation: The movement of material in solution inside the body of the plant. [NIH]

Transmitter: A chemical substance which effects the passage of nerve impulses from one cell to the other at the synapse. [NIH]

Trichotillomania: Compulsion to pull out one's hair. [NIH]

Tricuspid Atresia: Absence of the orifice between the right atrium and ventricle, with the presence of an atrial defect through which all the systemic venous return reaches the left heart. As a result, there is left ventricular hypertrophy because the right ventricle is absent or not functional. [NIH]

Tricyclic: Containing three fused rings or closed chains in the molecular structure. [EU]

Tryptophan: An essential amino acid that is necessary for normal growth in infants and for nitrogen balance in adults. It is a precursor serotonin and niacin. [NIH]

Tyramine: An indirect sympathomimetic. Tyramine does not directly activate adrenergic receptors, but it can serve as a substrate for adrenergic uptake systems and monoamine oxidase so it prolongs the actions of adrenergic transmitters. It also provokes transmitter release from adrenergic terminals. Tyramine may be a neurotransmitter in some invertebrate nervous systems. [NIH]

Tyrosine: A non-essential amino acid. In animals it is synthesized from phenylalanine. It is also the precursor of epinephrine, thyroid hormones, and melanin. [NIH]

Ulcer: A localized necrotic lesion of the skin or a mucous surface. [NIH]

Unconscious: Experience which was once conscious, but was subsequently rejected, as the "personal unconscious". [NIH]

Urethra: The tube through which urine leaves the body. It empties urine from the bladder. [NIH]

Urine: Fluid containing water and waste products. Urine is made by the kidneys, stored in the bladder, and leaves the body through the urethra. [NIH]

Uterus: The small, hollow, pear-shaped organ in a woman's pelvis. This is the organ in which a fetus develops. Also called the womb. [NIH]

Vaccine: A substance or group of substances meant to cause the immune system to respond to a tumor or to microorganisms, such as bacteria or viruses. [NIH]

Vagina: The muscular canal extending from the uterus to the exterior of the body. Also called the birth canal. [NIH]

Vaginal: Of or having to do with the vagina, the birth canal. [NIH]

Vascular: Pertaining to blood vessels or indicative of a copious blood supply. [EU]

Vasodilator: An agent that widens blood vessels. [NIH]

Vector: Plasmid or other self-replicating DNA molecule that transfers DNA between cells in nature or in recombinant DNA technology. [NIH]

Venous: Of or pertaining to the veins. [EU]

Ventricle: One of the two pumping chambers of the heart. The right ventricle receives oxygen-poor blood from the right atrium and pumps it to the lungs through the pulmonary artery. The left ventricle receives oxygen-rich blood from the left atrium and pumps it to the body through the aorta. [NIH]

Ventricular: Pertaining to a ventricle. [EU]

Vesicular: 1. Composed of or relating to small, saclike bodies. 2. Pertaining to or made up of vesicles on the skin. [EU]

Veterinary Medicine: The medical science concerned with the prevention, diagnosis, and treatment of diseases in animals. [NIH]

Viral: Pertaining to, caused by, or of the nature of virus. [EU]

Virulence: The degree of pathogenicity within a group or species of microorganisms or viruses as indicated by case fatality rates and/or the ability of the organism to invade the tissues of the host. [NIH]

Virus: Submicroscopic organism that causes infectious disease. In cancer therapy, some viruses may be made into vaccines that help the body build an immune response to, and kill, tumor cells. [NIH]

Vitro: Descriptive of an event or enzyme reaction under experimental investigation occurring outside a living organism. Parts of an organism or microorganism are used together with artificial substrates and/or conditions. [NIH]

Vivo: Outside of or removed from the body of a living organism. [NIH]

Vulva: The external female genital organs, including the clitoris, vaginal lips, and the opening to the vagina. [NIH]

War: Hostile conflict between organized groups of people. [NIH]

Xenograft: The cells of one species transplanted to another species. [NIH]

INDEX

Printed in the United States
150522LV00001B/84/A

9 780597 836053